What people are saying about …

UNFAITHFUL

"This is an outstanding book that offers a real-world Christian perspective on how adultery can happen in any marriage, no matter what the existing circumstance. The honesty and transparency the Shrivers share in this story will help couples see how God can heal marriages, even those on the verge of destruction and headed for divorce."

Mitch Temple, director of marriage
at Focus on the Family

"*Practical, insightful,* and *healing* are the words to describe this resource. Blending their personal journey with helpful guidelines for recovery, this book can be a redeeming tool for broken marriages."

H. Norman Wright, author,
grief and trauma therapist

"Using their own story as a rich backdrop, Gary and Mona Shriver provide couples with valuable stepping stones for crossing the torrent of pain that occurs with marital infidelity. Couples will find hope and help in their healing as they are encouraged that marriage can not only survive, but thrive after an affair."

Michael Sytsma, PhD, nationally certified
counselor and sex therapist, director of
Building Intimate Marriages, Inc.

"With honesty and clarity, the Shrivers give hope and help to the hurting couple. To love again is possible with the Shrivers' help.

Bill and Pam Farrel, best-selling authors
of *Men Are Like Waffles, Women Are Like
Spaghetti* and *The Marriage Code*

"Gary and Mona understand the process of recovering from infidelity as well as anyone I know. This updated edition of *Unfaithful* is a realistic, practical, and extremely helpful resource for anyone on that journey. This is one of the main books we recommend to people facing this difficult issue."

Robert S. Paul, copresident of the National
Institute of Marriage and coauthor of the
best-selling *The DNA of Relationships*

"This book is incredibly impactful. Gary and Mona unveil their deepest, most inner thoughts around the crisis they faced and how they processed it to reach the place of healing. It is a must-read for those who serve and minister to individuals and couples dealing with infidelity, but will undoubtedly make an impact on all couples by showing how important it is to guard your hearts and marriage."

Eric and Jennifer Garcia, founders
of the Association of Marriage and
Family Ministries (AMFM)

"Gary and Mona are the real deal! They pull back the veil and share their experiences with transparency and authenticity. Anyone who works with couples in trouble needs to read this book. It will give you an incredible understanding into the hearts of those to whom you minister. And if you are struggling in your marriage, this book will give you hope that you can rebuild your marriage."

Greg Braly, pastor of family ministries
at New Hope Church and national
director of family ministries for the
Evangelical Free Church of America

"As a practicing therapist treating infidelity, I have found *Unfaithful* to be one of the best resources available. Both spouses will feel understood and enlightened."

Rick Reynolds, LCSW, founder of the Affair
Recovery Center and national spokesman

"Finally! For thirty years, I have been looking for this book! Although it is a story of one couple's recovery from adultery, it is the best affair-prevention book I know of."

Dave Carder, MFT, pastor of counseling
ministries at First Evangelical Free Church
and author of *Torn Asunder* and *Close Calls*

"The Shrivers share their thoughts, their feelings, and their choices so that others may have a roadmap to follow to recovery."

Sherman R. Glenn, licensed
marriage and family therapist

unfaithful

*un*faithful

Hope and Healing After Infidelity

Gary and Mona Shriver

David C Cook®

transforming lives together

UNFAITHFUL
Published by David C. Cook
4050 Lee Vance View
Colorado Springs, CO 80918 U.S.A.

David C. Cook Distribution Canada
55 Woodslee Avenue, Paris, Ontario, Canada N3L 3E5

David C. Cook U.K., Kingsway Communications
Eastbourne, East Sussex BN23 6NT, England

David C. Cook and the graphic circle C logo
are registered trademarks of Cook Communications Ministries.

The Web site addresses recommended throughout this book are offered as a
resource to you. These Web sites are not intended in any way to be or imply an
endorsement on the part of David C. Cook, nor do we vouch for their content.

All Scripture quotations, unless otherwise noted, are taken from the *Holy Bible, New
International Version*®. *NIV*®. Copyright © 1973, 1978, 1984 by International Bible
Society. Used by permission of Zondervan. All rights reserved. Scripture quotations
marked NASB are taken from the *New American Standard Bible*, © Copyright 1960,
1995 by The Lockman Foundation. Used by permission; NLT are taken from the New
Living Translation of the Holy Bible. New Living Translation copyright © 1996,
2004 by Tyndale Charitable Trust. Used by permission of Tyndale House Publishers.
Quiz material at the end of chapter 12 is reprinted by permission of International
Creative Management, Inc. Copyright © 2003 by Shirley Glass.

LCCN 2009907121
ISBN 978-1-4347-6533-8
eISBN 978-0-7814-0440-2

© 2009 Gary and Mona Shriver
First edition published by Life Journey © 2005 Gary and
Mona Shriver, ISBN 978-0-7814-4268-8

The Team: Susan Tjaden, Amy Kiechlin, Jack Campbell, and Karen Athen
Cover Design: Sarah Schultz
Cover Photo: Veer, Inc.

Printed in the United States of America
Second Edition 2009

3 4 5 6 7 8 9 10

010311

Contents

Acknowledgments

We must first acknowledge a God whose love for us is greater than all our sin—our Lord who provides the hope and healing we human beings are so in need of. May we be His good and faithful servants.

To our counselor and brother, Sherman Glenn. Your guidance kept us on the path of healing. You not only heard our cries but also facilitated the forming of a ministry we so desperately needed ourselves. We are humbled by the trust you placed in us as you allowed us to come alongside other couples.

To Mike and Jo, who walked with us and are the cofounders of Hope & Healing Ministries. We would never have chosen this path to a friendship, but your validation, willing hearts, and encouragement so beautifully illustrate Romans 8:28. We can only pray the four of us will continue in ministry together for many more years.

To our prayer team. You are faithful members of the body of Christ. Some of you upheld us in the early days of our own crisis, and some came later as God led. We do not underestimate your value. God alone knows the work you have done for us personally and for the ministry we are privileged to be a part of.

To the couples who have participated with us in our Hope & Healing support groups. Your courage and strength are to be admired—you did not take the easy path. Thank you for opening yourselves up to us and for the many lessons you have taught us.

To Mary McNeil, who sat on a bench with us at Mount Hermon and believed our message was worth hearing. We believe God chose you to be His instrument in making this book a reality, and every reader will be blessed by the improvements you made in our manuscript. Those readers will never know what you did, but we do. It has been a privilege.

Foreword

In an age where marriage scandal is blared from every newspaper and TV set, Christians are strangely silent about their scandals.

In an age where vulnerability is the mark of the times, Christians are not willing to be vulnerable.

In an age where divorce is the common answer to adultery, Christians must declare, "There can be hope and healing!" In *Unfaithful*, Mona and Gary Shriver shout, *"There is hope! Healing can come to your marriage!"*

With gut-wrenching honesty, Mona and Gary open the most painful portion of their lives to you—the part labeled betrayal. No candy-coated answers are given. Pain, heartache, hopelessness, anger, and exhaustion all march across these pages. No simplistic answers are offered. Mona and Gary never say working through the horror of adultery is easy. What they do offer you is one couple's journey beginning with the revelation of betrayal through every stage of healing. You will discover how Mona and Gary found strength to endure the pain, how they learned to honestly acknowledge their losses, wrestle through forgiveness, and finally build hedges around their renewed relationship.

If you are walking through the pain of unfaithfulness, buy this book. If a friend is in the agony of betrayal, buy this book for him or her. We promise you will be lifted on wings of hope to the Healer and given practical help that can bring healing. We highly recommend this book!

Dr. Joseph and Linda Dillow
Dr. Peter and Lorraine Pintus
Authors of Intimacy Ignited *and* Intimate Issues

Preface to Revision

When *Unfaithful* was originally published, we both believed we were following God one baby step at a time. We had no idea what His plan was or how the book might play a role in the healing of a couple dealing with infidelity. What we did believe was that there were people out there struggling and looking for hope as they tried to walk an unknown path toward healing their marriage. This belief had been confirmed by the local couples we were privileged to come alongside over the previous eight years through the peer support ministry we cofounded, Hope & Healing. Every decision Hope & Healing made has been preceded by this question: "How does it help the couples?" In the case of the original *Unfaithful*, it made our story of hope and some practical tools available to more couples. The decision to revise was also faced with this same question.

We thought about those who contacted us after reading the book. Husbands and wives letting us know God was using *Unfaithful* to bring a sense of hope into their world that had spun out of control. Multitudes of emails from all over this country and beyond every year validate that *Unfaithful* is a tool God uses to encourage those on this difficult road.

The point is that we know you are out there looking for resources and hope. And in the past few years, we have learned more about this recovery process through conferences and people who work with couples on a professional basis. We have grown. And we think we have more to share with you that could also be used to help your recovery process.

As a nonprofit ministry, our team is seeking to provide the best resources we can for those in recovery. Our goal is to extend the reach of our peer-to-peer support. God continues to bring hurting couples and potential facilitators into our groups. We also get requests for groups or support couples in other geographic areas. Hope & Healing is reproducing itself, so adding more useful information to *Unfaithful* benefits that reproduction.

The third factor in our decision is more personal. When *Unfaithful* was first published, we were uncomfortable with the potential exposure of our private life. Neither of us wanted to focus on the worst time in our lives. Yet we believe God called us to be the "face" for this ministry, and we have been obedient. We no longer fear exposure.

We are completely willing to go where God leads and to serve Him openly and proudly in this ministry.

God does nothing without cause. He wastes nothing.

> *Surely, as I have planned, so it will be, and*
> *as I have purposed, so it will stand.*
> *—Isaiah 14:24*

God did not plan for adultery, but we do believe He planned for how He would use it to benefit His kingdom. We will follow His lead.

Gary and Mona Shriver

1

Revelation

He reveals the deep things of darkness
and brings deep shadows into the light.

Job 12:22

GARY'S STORY

It must have been about 9:30 p.m. as I pulled into the driveway. Everything looked dark and settled down for the evening. As I stopped the car, my heart pounded in my chest like never before. For a moment I wondered if I might be having a heart attack. I took a deep breath, got out of the car, and headed for the back door. I unlocked it and walked onto the back porch. The house was quiet. The three boys were in bed. The only light was a dim glow from the master bedroom at the end of the hall.

Our bedroom. I wondered if that would be the case in the aftermath of the bomb I was about to drop. I stopped and asked myself, *Should I really go through with this?* This could be the end of everything I know as my life: my family, my church, my business, my friends. Not one area of my life would be unaffected by the event about to occur. *Should I tell her or just keep living the lie?*

No, I couldn't continue deceiving her. I had just spent the last two hours in my senior pastor's office confessing my sin. I confessed the double life I had been living for the last few years. I couldn't believe his first response. "Are you serious?" he asked. "I can never tell when you're kidding me. Are you really serious?" I sat in his office with tears streaming down my face, and he asked if I was serious.

He also didn't want it to be true.

I just nodded, and he let it sink in. We talked and prayed, and he kept looking at me. I knew what was going through his mind. He was saying great words of spiritual wisdom and offering encouragement, but behind his words, shock and disbelief were apparent. He referred to spiritual leaders who had fallen. He said, "This is happening all around us."

At that point, I could only think, *That doesn't make this any less ugly.* I knew he was trying to encourage and comfort me in my darkest hour, but the darkness that enveloped me was beyond penetration. He and I both knew that everything was not all right and that it wasn't going to be.

He asked if Mona knew. I shook my head no. He looked me straight in the eye and asked, "Do you intend to tell her?"

I nodded.

"When?"

"Right now," I said. "I need to go right now."

It had taken all I could muster to meet my pastor and confess my dark and horrible behavior. I had to complete my confession. And I had to do it now. On my way home I thought of other men I knew who had committed adultery and who hadn't said a thing to their wives. They seemed to have gotten away with it. But a Bible verse kept ringing in my ears: "You may be sure that your sin will find you out" (Numbers 32:23).

And that it had. Earlier that afternoon the recording studio engineer at my production company had confronted me with this "problem" he thought I had. He came quoting Matthew 18:15–17, saying that if I didn't come clean, he would go to my pastor with the affair he believed I was having.

Affair. What a fluffy word. It sounds so cheery and acceptable. Let's call it what it really is: *adultery.* Black-hearted, not caring anything about anybody else, completely self-centered, the absolute epitome of selfishness. Adultery. And I was an adulterer. Finally after years of my wrestling with Him, God had brought me to a point of brokenness. I just couldn't go on like this anymore. I had to tell Mona. The only way I could ever hope to save my marriage was to be totally honest. God was chasing me. I had to deal with it now!

I walked into the bedroom. The lamp on her bedside table glowed. There she lay, leaning back on her pillow propped up against the wall, reading. She looked up and said, "How was your meeting?" Just about then our eyes met. "Honey? What's wrong?"

I hadn't rehearsed anything. I didn't know what to say. I sat down on the bed next to her and looked in her eyes.

"You're scaring me," she said.

I started to cry.

"Now you're really scaring me."

"I've betrayed you," I whispered.

Her eyes glazed over. She seemed to stare through me. "What?"

"I've been unfaithful to you," I repeated.

She went limp. I thought for a second she was going to pass out. Her stare went from distant to direct and cold.

"Who?" she demanded.

I said the name.

"I knew it," she said.

But I knew she hadn't known. I tried to hold her. She started to hold me but then pushed me away. She was shell-shocked.

"How long?" she asked.

I whispered, "A long time."

"How long?"

"A couple of years."

"Years? Ever since you started working with her?"

"Almost."

Her lip quivered.

As her world crumbled around her feet, my heart raced again. This time I could feel it in my temples. How could I say more? *How can I, Lord? I can't tell her everything.* Yet God was insistent: *Tell her!*

I felt like Moses must have. *I can't, Lord. I can't!*

Tell her now! God demanded.

I had to tell her everything. God burned into my heart that if our marriage were to have any chance at all, it had to be with a clean slate. No more lies. No more secrets. I had to tell her everything.

"There's more."

"More? What do you mean more?"

"There was a one-night stand with another woman."

I honestly did think she was going to pass out at that point. Her eyes rolled back into her head, and then things got eerie.

I knew at that moment our lives had changed forever, and I didn't know what to expect in the aftermath of my horrible revelation. After we sat for what seemed to be an eternity, her blank stare suddenly focused, and the flurry of questions began. "Do you love her?"

"No, I love you."

"Do you want a divorce?"

"No, I want to stay with you. Do you want a divorce?"

"I don't know what I want. Why did you do this?"

I didn't know how to answer that question. I didn't know how I'd gotten where I was. I explained there had been no pursuit. I said that it was a friendship that had gotten out of control, and that I had felt trapped. I had never stopped loving Mona.

The blank stare was back. I kept trying to explain. She didn't want to hear—or couldn't hear—anything more. After a while she started asking me about the second woman.

"It was a one-night thing. Honestly, she threw herself at me. She made up her mind to have me. She set her sights, and she was going to have her way."

What was I saying? It was all the truth, but what was I trying to do here? Justify my adultery? My *second* incidence of adultery at that!

I shut my mouth and started to cry again. I didn't know what to do. She didn't want to talk about it anymore. She didn't want anything from me. I was dying inside. I needed to know what she was thinking. She was in shock. Was she thinking of leaving? Was she going to ask me to leave? What was going on in her head?

It seemed there was nothing more to say. I offered to sleep on the couch, but she declined my offer. She explained that if we were going to try to work this through, she saw no sense in my sleeping on the couch.

If. Such a small word to hold one's whole future.

It was quiet and still, but I knew the explosion was yet to come. She stared blankly into the corner of the ceiling. I lay there, knowing her mind was whirling. I was sure her thoughts were bouncing from one horrific scenario to another, and all I could do was lie next to her and watch as her entire foundation cracked, crumbled, and fell away. Every now and then I could hear a sob escape her throat.

My God, what have I done? In a matter of seconds I have ripped the heart from the woman I love. The bride of my youth. Will she ever forgive me? Can she ever forgive me? I had no idea how much pain this would cause. If we make it through this, one thing is certain: We will never be the same again.

God, please forgive me.

Mona, if you can find it in your heart, please try to forgive me.

Mona's Story

I don't remember what book I was reading, but I do remember I never finished it. I threw it away. It would always remind me of that night.

I heard the back door open and thought, *Gary's home a little early—must have been a short meeting.*

I heard him walk down the hallway. He opened the bedroom door and just stood there, staring at me.

I said something like, "How'd your meeting go?" I watched as my husband of more than nineteen years began to crumble. His body sagged as if under a heavy weight.

His eyes filled with tears and he said, "We have to talk."

I knew something was terribly wrong and remember thinking someone had died. *I wonder if it's our pastor. He must have found out something horrible at the church meeting.* Compassion overwhelmed my heart, and I reached out my arms, inviting him in. "Oh, honey, what's wrong?"

He came to the bed, sat down by me, and allowed me to hold him while sobs racked his body. I had never seen him like this. Through his muffled tears I heard, "I have betrayed you."

I felt my body stiffen. A tragedy had happened, not to someone else, but to me. My mind refused to process his words. "What?"

"I have been having an affair."

These words penetrated, and I felt my own tears rise. I heard the word come from my mouth before I realized I had even thought it: "Who?"

Why was there no surprise when he said her name? I remember even then knowing there was really only one true possibility. I also remember other names going through my head, almost hoping he'd say one of those instead. I had never suspected. I trusted them both implicitly. He was my husband, whom I loved and who I thought loved me. She was his coworker, a fellow church member, and the woman I had considered my best Christian friend for the past three or four years.

"How long?" I asked.

"Awhile," he mumbled.

I began to feel the first stirring of rage. *"How long?"*

"A couple of years maybe."

Not just once or even twice. Not a few weeks or even a few months! Was I a complete idiot? How could something like this go on for so long and I not even have a clue? They must have thought I was so stupid! How many times had they laughed at my naïveté?

I pulled away from him, unable to touch him, unable to do much more than breathe.

Then I heard these words: "There's more."

More? More than the destruction of my life, my family, my church, my home? *More?*

"I also had a one-night stand with another woman." Then he named her, a twenty-year-old single mother and non-Christian with whom we'd had business dealings.

"She came over one night uninvited when you were gone."

Here? In my house? Nothing was sacred. Every aspect of my life was involved. My home. The church where I always sat with my best friend. Gary's production business where I worked part-time. Even the hospital where I worked as a nurse was filled with people who crossed over into these aspects of my life.

I was nauseous. Repulsed. This was something horrible men did. Not my Gary! Not the man I had always jokingly said I'd have to catch in bed naked before I'd ever believe he'd be unfaithful. The man couldn't lie for beans.

Gary was not the man I had thought he was, but I was no longer sure who I was either. For that matter, who were we as a couple? Were we a couple?

I looked at him and froze. This was the man I'd been married to for almost twenty years. He'd been my lover, my best friend, and my confidant. My family loved him because he was so wonderful. All my friends thought he was wonderful—he did dishes, laundry, and changed diapers. I had lost count of how many times I'd been told how lucky I was.

My body was numb, wooden, overwhelmed. The weight Gary had walked into our bedroom wearing was now being shared.

"Do you love her?"

"No."

"Do you want a divorce?"

"No."

"Does her husband know?"

"I think she's waiting to see if I really tell you first."

"You have to let her go."

"I know."

The particulars of our conversation blur in retrospect. He told me he had gone to the church to confess to our pastor. The pastor had called in another pastor, they had all prayed, and then they sent Gary home to tell me.

He told me that the recording studio engineer had confronted him that day. He had suspected what was going on and had gone to his pastor, who advised him to confront Gary. What strength that must have taken for such a young man!

Gary said God had been preparing him for this revelation for a long time. Promise Keepers, meetings, sermons, his conscience. He had felt trapped in the relationship with his coworker for quite a while. If he broke it off, he knew the ramifications and the possibility of losing his family, his business, and his church. They had broken it off many times in the past and yet would find themselves back together. He couldn't remember when it started, but the last time they'd been together was just three days earlier. I remembered trying to reach him that day. They had gone out of town to see a client and I'd wondered why they were so late getting back.

As I tried to pin down the time period of the affair, it became clear that it had been going on for about three years. It began shortly after she started working with us. Her marriage was in trouble and had been for a very long time. She and I had talked about it often together. I felt like such a fool. Gary and I had even discussed her vulnerability and her attractiveness before they started working together. I knew she envied our relationship, but I hadn't realized that she had actually been wishing for Gary himself. She, as it turned out, knew better than I what my marriage was really like.

That night my life took on a new timetable: before the affair, during the affair, and after the affair. Everything during was now marred and distorted: our family trip to Disneyland, Gary and I going to Hawaii. I recalled snippets of conversation with both Gary and my friend and suddenly heard and saw completely different things.

He asked me that night if I would come to work for him full-time at our production company and we'd rebuild our lives and the business. I was furious. How dare he! I told him I wasn't going to give up any more of me than he'd already ripped away. I was a nurse. I was a good nurse. I couldn't lose that, too.

He asked me if I wanted a divorce, and I said no. What would that do to our boys? Where would I go? What would I do?

We talked about counseling. To what end? I was so overwhelmed that even counseling seemed senseless. I wanted it never to have happened and a counselor couldn't do that.

Gary told me about the night the young woman had come over and seduced him. He said it was very intentional on her part. I said that did not exonerate him. He knew that. The story of that one-night stand sounded like a despicable movie.

Soon it seemed there was nothing left to talk about. Or maybe it was just that we were incapable of talking anymore. Gary reassured me that he loved me and wished he could take it all away. He asked for my forgiveness and told me he'd do anything I asked. I knew that adultery was biblical grounds for divorce, but I didn't know if that still applied when the offender repents and asks for forgiveness.

My mind, soul, and body were exhausted by the events of the night. I knew I wanted to follow God in this, no matter where that led. I knew I needed a godly friend and felt again the pain of loss. Who would I call now that my two best friends had betrayed me?

When we went to bed, Gary asked if I wanted him to sleep somewhere else. I said no. I figured he'd been in my bed during the last three years, so what difference would it make now?

And so I clung to my edge of the bed and listened to my husband fall into a deep and restful sleep. Sleep would evade me. I would spend most of what was left of that night in the family room crying.

Gary's weight had begun to lift. Mine had only just begun to press heavily upon me.

The Story on Revelation

That night happened in 1993. We can now say with absolute sincerity that we have fully healed from the adultery. Our marriage is strong and mutually satisfying. We have love and trust.

We refuse, however, to say that our marriage is better. We had heard "now they have a better marriage" in reference to couples who had gone through serious problems, and it only caused us more pain. We'd thought our marriage was good before the adultery. We loved each other; we were best friends. Certainly we had issues; all couples do. But our marriage prior to the adultery had value and was good. What happened to us happened to a good marriage. Most people have a hard time believing that because if they do, it makes every marriage vulnerable—including their own. Certainly there are those instances when the whys and wherefores are clear, but often all the answers we seek cannot be found. So instead we say we are wiser than we were then. We make better choices now. And we no longer believe we are invulnerable to attack. Our marriage is better only because the two people in it are now better people.

♥

If you have picked up this book, you are probably going through, or love someone going through, the aftermath of finding out about a spouse's adultery. Our hearts break for you, and we want you to know there is hope. Marriages can heal. We know because ours did. We know because we've been able to support other couples facing this anguish. We also know it will be one of the hardest things you will ever go through. We believe it would have been far easier *at the time* for us to split up. And we would not have been condemned for doing so. That same thing is true for many others.

We know these words seem hard to believe. When you go through this crisis, you feel as if the weight of the world is pressing down on you. Then the fiery darts from hell come faster and faster, and your shield of faith seems to offer little protection. You are fighting for your marriage with every ounce of strength you can muster until you begin to fear you're going to lose the battle. This is where Satan wants you, and he will be faithful to keep the burners on high. Why? He wants nothing more than to see your marriage fail. He wants you to become another statistic. So let us repeat ourselves: You don't have to give up! You can make it!

How? We want to share with you what made the difference. We were Christians when the adultery happened. We are still Christians. What we will share with you is definitely from a Christian perspective, but it is also from a practical, real-life perspective.

Is our marriage now perfect? No. We still have issues, and we've learned that some will remain until we get to heaven. Perhaps we've learned to pick our battles with more grace and wisdom. We have also learned that some battles were due to our own selfish desires and were far removed from the marriage partnership.

We are not, nor do we claim to be, experts in anything. We have no educational or professional background to validate us. Those people are out there, and their resources are available to you. You'll need them, too. But if you seek two ordinary believers to share their extraordinary experience, then here we are. We do not undertake this task lightly. This is not our idea of fun. In the early stages of writing, our emotions often overwhelmed us, and there were times we would leave our desks sobbing. We found ourselves crying over things we hadn't cried over in years. Our God, however, is a great God and gracious to His people. In time we felt that we were merely observing a sad story, rather than reliving the awful past.

GETTING THE MOST FROM THE REST OF THIS BOOK

Terminology

Before we start sharing with you our own story and healing process, we need to establish a common language. Many have different ways of identifying people and moments in time when talking about adultery. Some are terms we wouldn't be allowed to print here. So, to get us on the same page, we'll define some terms and provide you with information that can help you walk through your recovery. Nothing about infidelity recovery is simple or easily explained, but there are definitely areas where, if both of you have the same understanding, you can avoid some common pitfalls.

First, the terminology for the cast of characters will be borrowed from the very practical book *Torn Asunder: Recovering from an Extramarital Affair* by Dave Carder:

> *Infidel: the one who strays and*
> > *gets involved in an illicit*
> > *relationship—it simply means*
> > *unfaithful.*
> *Spouse: the one married to the infidel.*
> *Partner: the person with whom the*
> > *infidel was involved.*[1]

A term we use often is *revelation*. This refers to the event where the infidel admits to the spouse that an illicit relationship has occurred. Sometimes the word is plural, *revelations,* because the full story takes more than one admission, as parts are revealed over time. *Revelation* is used throughout the book as a reference point.

Finally, the adulterous relationship will be referred to as *an affair* with the disclaimer that the word sounds much too playful for the seriousness of this offense.

We also need to agree on what adultery is. That might sound pretty silly to a lot of you, but differing on what comprises adultery can cause some serious problems. In fact, former President Clinton provided us with a classic example of what constituted "sex" when he denied having sex with another woman, yet later admitted to sexual intimacies with that woman. We can only imagine the private conversations he had with his wife when the truth was revealed.

We've heard some infidels deny adultery because they didn't have sexual intercourse even while admitting there was sexual contact. They admit what they did was wrong but do not call it adultery.

As a matter of fact, the dictionary definition of adultery states it just that way: "Voluntary sexual intercourse between a married person and a partner other than the lawful spouse."[2] *Infidelity* is defined as a lack of loyalty to one's spouse.[3] By the *adultery* definition, President Clinton was correct. By the *infidelity* definition, any number of things could fall into that category—anything a spouse would consider disloyal. Looking exclusively at either dictionary definition allows one to go to opposing ends of the spectrum of possibilities.

While the dictionary may disagree, *for our purposes adultery and infidelity will be equivalent terms.* The truth is that there is no one clear and concise definition of infidelity or adultery that everyone agrees on.

We'll define adultery as *unfaithfulness to the covenant (i.e., marriage) vows you made to your spouse.* Vows are the promises we make to one another when we stand before God and whomever else to become legally wed. We promise (vow) to love, honor, and cherish the person we are marrying. We promise this person that they are now the number one person in our life, even if our health and wealth and other circumstances change.

We also vow to forsake all others. That means we have reserved the intimacy space of the marriage relationship *exclusively* for the person we married. Anytime we put another person in that relational space promised to our partner—be it sexual or emotional or both—we have committed adultery. We have violated the intimacy of marriage, we have broken our promise, and we have had an illicit relationship.

We love the description Dr. Shirley Glass gives in *Not "Just Friends"*:

> In a committed relationship [marriage], a couple constructs a wall that shields them from any outside forces that have the power to split them. They look at the world outside their relationship through a shared window of openness and honesty. The couple is a unit, and they have a

united front to deal with children, in-laws, and friends. An affair erodes their carefully constructed security system. It erects an interior *wall of secrecy* between the marriage partners, at the same time it opens a *window of intimacy* between the affair partners. The couple is no longer a unit. The affair partner is on the inside, and the marital partner is on the outside.[4]

And here is the true acid test. It's simple. It's easy. It's three words: *Ask your spouse.* Explain everything about your other relationship. Be 100 percent honest about every detail, thought, and touch. Then ask your spouse. They'll be able to tell you if it fits the definition of adultery in a heartbeat.

Time Frame of Chapters

What we are sharing with you is not chronological. Quite frankly, healing isn't that neat. And often many of us wander in and out of these areas throughout the recovery process. So rather, we have chosen to share with you by topics: those areas we needed to explore and deal with as we healed. We hope all of you will deal with each principle area, but the truth is that none of you will do it at the same time. *When* you encounter each principle area will be determined by who you are, what type of affair you're dealing with, and the journey our Lord has you on.

We do, however, believe the first two principle areas, commitment and faith, are foundational. So if you need to camp out there for a while, that is okay. These two areas will provide the sure footing you'll need to walk through the rest.

We can relate only our experience and a glimpse at others we have known. Yours will be entirely different, but we are certain that you, like the couples in our groups, will find some value in the sharing. Seek other godly counsel and ask God Himself to help you filter through and apply what is right for your situation.

When we were in the deepest pit of our crisis, we wanted to sit across from a couple whose marriage had survived this horror and who now had a marriage they both cherished. Someone who could look us straight in the eye and tell us we could make it because they had. Someone who could help us understand we weren't crazy but rather experiencing a horrendous crisis—validating what was normal for the abnormal situation in which we found ourselves. This is what we'll offer you.

♥

Now, come with us and we'll take you along through snapshots of our journey of healing. We'll give you some ideas and concrete suggestions as to how some of these things we've talked about can look. We pray you'll see truth, reality, and hope, and that God will use what we share to help you on your journey.

We have seen the Lord do marvelous things, and we will pray those same marvelous things for you.

> *Praise be to the God and Father of our Lord*
> *Jesus Christ, the Father of compassion and*
> *the God of all comfort, who comforts us in*

all our troubles, so that we can comfort those in any trouble with the comfort we ourselves have received from God. For just as the sufferings of Christ flow over into our lives, so also through Christ our comfort overflows.

—2 Corinthians 1:3–5

2
Commitment

*Commit your way to the LORD; trust in
him and he will do this: He will make
your righteousness shine like the dawn, the
justice of your cause like the noonday sun.*

Psalm 37:5–6

MONA'S STORY
(Less than six months after revelation)

Please, God, let me have a happy marriage. That was my prayer from
the time I was little. I knew early on that I didn't want my marriage
to be like that of my parents, who had very little happiness together.
I do remember a brief time when I was ten that seemed to be happy.
It was right after a move. Dad had a good job, Mom was able to stay
home, and we lived in a nice house in a good area. Soon, however,
things reverted to what was normal for us—Dad too sick to work,
Mom working, and another move into a worse house. Both of them

miserable. Still, I had that brief glimpse of what I thought should be a normal home, one where everyone liked each other. I wanted that for myself when I grew up and had my own family.

When things went well with my family, we went to church. When they did not, we did not. Attendance seemed to be associated with our circumstances and not with our desire to worship God. The church we attended was legalistic; entrance to heaven was determined by how well you obeyed the rules. By the time I was a teenager, I knew I couldn't obey all the rules. Because I was going to hell, I determined to have fun here on earth while I could. I rejected the church, God, and anything or anybody religious. However, the childish prayer of a young girl stayed with me. *Please, God, let me have a happy marriage.*

That prayer seemed to be answered when Gary and I married in May of 1974. I was twenty and he was twenty-one. Neither one of us was a believer. He hadn't been raised in any church or religion. Both of us had left home at eighteen, had worked since we were young, and were pretty responsible.

In 1979, a friend of Gary's came to see him. He shared his story of recent salvation and faith, and before he left, he gave Gary a Bible and "prayed the prayer" with him. When I got home, Gary informed me of what had happened. I scoffed. *He just doesn't know what this is all about like I do,* I thought. I'm sure my negative expression and body language clearly said that this was a subject we were not going to discuss. Gary wisely made no changes in our lifestyle. He did begin to read that Bible, although he had no follow-up or formal discipleship opportunities. On the rare occasion when the subject of faith came up, I would again scoff and tell him he was going to hell right along with me for all the things he continued to do—like smoking, drinking, and cussing. Satan had also been faithful to provide us with another friend who thought the same way I did. Gary didn't argue much; he would just look at us and say that wasn't what he was reading in the Bible.

Time went on, and God pursued me. He used many things over the next three years to soften my heart and expose my need. Finally in 1982, I determined to read the Bible for myself and resolve this issue once and for all. I started in Matthew and read straight through the New Testament. By the time I got to Romans 7, I had said yes to God's truth. However, with very little reverence, I announced to Him that He was going to have to prove it to me.

He did then. And He still does today.

Seven years later I was feeling a spiritual hunger not yet satisfied. I began an inductive Bible study, and my whole life changed. I saw truth. I learned I could understand truth and discern error. For most of my life I had run from a God I'd been told about, not from a God I knew.

The peace and the freedom were exciting.

The understanding that I would be accountable for what I knew was frightening.

The desire to continue learning was like nothing I'd ever experienced. So God took those next few years and taught me. During that process, I made a commitment to Him. I would never leave or run again, no matter what. That commitment has been tested with some painful difficulties, but it has held fast.

♥

I tell you all this to help you understand what a big part this played in my response to Gary's adultery. God had taught me truth—His truth. I had chosen to believe and obey, and I knew that my obedience would often be the opposite of what I felt like doing. It did not make what Gary and I went through any easier, but I really felt I had no choice other than to walk through it. I simply did not have release from my heavenly Father to seriously consider divorce. It wasn't an option. We had three young children who would either benefit by our ability to recover or pay dearly if we split up. That's the spiritual reason. The other reasons are not so spiritual.

First, there was pride. I was proud of my happy marriage. I knew so many who did not have one, and I had been fortunate. There was no way I was going to throw that all away. I valued it. And Gary seemed to want to rebuild it. Therefore, I would try.

Second, there was more pride. People so often think there are good guys and bad guys in marriage. It's easy to observe couples, watch the dynamics, and get a glimpse of who's the easier one to live with. I've already told you my family loved Gary. He was easygoing and fun, loving, talented, a giver by nature. Most of the wives were jealous, and most of the men gave him a bad time for making them look bad. Who do you think most people thought was the "better one"? Even under the circumstances of adultery, when it was all said and done, I knew that most would end up understanding him.

Third, I really didn't have anywhere else to go. I had never been as close in spirit with anyone else as I was with my husband. That "good marriage" had provided me with an intimate partner, one I took all my troubles to, a friend I could go to with anything and he would still love me and help me through it. I was going through hell. I knew it wasn't going to be over quickly. I had a choice: I could go through it alone, or I could go through it with Gary.

♥

I was sitting on the couch after another day of pain. A few months had passed since Gary's revelation; most of it was a blur. I was tired of hiding my pain from the world. On the days I worked at the hospital, it took everything I had just to make it through my shift without breaking down. One of the girls had walked into the break room and, looking straight at me, said, "You look like you just lost your best friend." I wanted to scream at her that I had in fact lost both of them, but I mumbled something benign instead and left the room. I was checking and rechecking every medication I gave, every order I completed because my mind was not working right. For the first time in my life, I experienced stress so severe it was incapacitating. I didn't know how much more I could take.

And there were the boys. Our oldest was withdrawing more and more. Our middle son was getting into constant trouble. And who had time for the youngest? I was not only a failure as a wife but a blatant failure as a mother also. I knew Gary was tired too, but this wasn't my fault. I didn't do this. He did it.

I heard Gary come in, and I heard the boys greet their father. Normal sounds. But this wasn't a normal household. Nothing was normal anymore. I wasn't normal. All I could do was cry and ask questions. I was obsessed. Everyone would be fine if I could just move on. They could all just live their normal little lives with all the other normal people.

I grabbed my car keys and ran out the door. I got in my van and just drove. I had to get away. Tears streamed down my face. Was I ever going to be able to stop crying? Was there never to be any relief from this hell? I screamed at God, *When is this going to be over? How could you allow this? Why didn't you protect us from this? Why? Why? Why?*

I didn't know where I was going. *I'm not even safe driving. Oh, God, just kill me and end this, please!* The name of a friend popped into my head, and I turned the car toward her house. About halfway there I thought of her husband and children. How could I go there and expose them to this? They didn't even know about it.

Another friend. She knew. I could go there. I turned in the opposite direction. She, too, had children. I couldn't go there. Her husband was a friend of Gary's. I couldn't do this to them.

I turned again. Where can I go? *Maybe I'll go to a bar. I'll get drunk and stay in a motel. Maybe I'll even pick up a man and see what it's like to commit adultery.* Even as I thought these things, I knew I couldn't go. I'd end up sick, or worse, I'd drive drunk and kill somebody else. Besides, if I committed adultery, we'd have to go through all the AIDS testing again, and I couldn't do that. A book I'd read said you should get tested after adultery. We discounted it at first, but when we stopped to consider the possibilities of whom Gary had been exposed to, it was frightening. And so we had Gary tested—one of life's most embarrassing moments. Filling out forms with questions such as, "How many sexual partners have you had in the last six months?" Knowing the tech who comes to draw your blood has read the answers. Then waiting for days, weeks. One night I dreamed the test came back positive, and then I was positive, and we had to tell the partner and her husband, and they were positive, and we were all dying and everyone knew why. At least that part was a nightmare from which I could wake up.

I drove aimlessly, going down lists of names in my mind. Who could I go to? Who would comfort me?

I thought of another friend, this one without children. I could go there. Then I remembered they weren't Christians, and God had impressed on me that those who would help me had to be Christians.

I stopped my van at the top of an overpass. I laid my head on the steering wheel and sobbed like a baby. There was no one. No one. No one I could lay this burden on and not be sorry later that I had done so. There was only one person who could truly help me and who needed to experience this with me. My husband.

As I turned the van to go home, I spoke again to God. *You're not going to let me go anywhere else, are you?* I had committed to Him and to Gary. One way or another, the three of us would see this thing through.

GARY'S STORY

(Less than six months after revelation)

I can honestly say that I always felt committed to Mona. "Yeah, right," you say. "Even during the affair?" I know it sounds weird, but I felt committed.

I had been surrounded by solid marriages all my life. I was raised in a small middle-class community in northern California.

If ever there was a "Beaver Cleaver" existence, I was raised in the midst of it. My folks were happy. I can't remember a fight or a harsh word between them. My grandparents were very much a part of our lives, and they always seemed more than happy. I wasn't raised in a Christian home, but morals and a sense of right and wrong were a part of my upbringing. I was brought up to believe that marriage was for life. It was something of value.

We didn't go to church very often during my childhood. I knew there was a God, and I had heard of Jesus, His Son, but I really didn't know anything about a relationship with Him.

As I left my teens and entered my twenties, I started to feel a tug on my heart. I really didn't know what to do about it, but there was a definite void.

When I was in my late twenties, a fellow musician I had lost contact with for a couple of years called one day. He had been writing songs and had heard I had a recording studio. He said he'd love to drive down and show me his work and maybe record a demo. A few days later, he was knocking on my door, ready to share these songs he had written about Jesus, his new personal Savior. I had known this guy well when we played in a band together, and he was no Christian then. As a matter of fact, he was quite the opposite. But he had really changed. He was much softer spoken and not nearly as pushy. He didn't use profanity once while we were together, and that was not like him at all. He shared his songs and his heart, and it wasn't more than a couple of sessions later that I found myself praying with him the prayer of salvation.

♥

So what's this all have to do with Mona and my commitment to our marriage?

I never really thought I was a prime candidate for adultery. Mona and I were happy. I was committed to our marriage, and I didn't think I was what you would call "high risk." So how did I get there?

The best description I ever heard was "baby steps." I let myself get into an intimate friendship with another female. Our conversations began innocently enough—family, friends, and ministry. But as time went on our friendship deepened. We started sharing more about ourselves and our lives. Our wants, our desires, our struggles. All the while, the underlying attraction was blooming as our constant contact fed it. One baby step led to another and to another, and before I could turn and run, I was in way too deep. The day she was sharing about something hurtful and began crying, I stood and offered a friendly shoulder. That offer of comfort became much more within seconds. Falling was much easier than I'd ever believed possible.

It was also at that point in our marriage that I was angry with Mona for putting me on the back burner of her priorities. I could point to many reasons why I was angry. The bottom line is that I felt she didn't want me in any way at all. But she was my wife. I loved her. I had made a commitment to her before God when we said our marriage vows. "I'm in for life," I always said.

My infidelity revealed the truth. But when God brought me to the point of brokenness and it was time to get this all out in the open, I felt a sense of commitment that I knew could come only from God. I would use all my strength to convince Mona I was here to stay, and nothing she could do or say would change that. And boy, did I find out that she could do and say plenty! It had to be God's strength that fashioned in me what I called "armadillo skin." She used words I had never heard her say before. But I was committed.

After a few months on this plane, I found out what commitment was all about. I had started out with a purposed and diligent attitude. I was there at all hours—and I mean all hours—with answers to her questions. I talked and explained until I ran out of words. And then I got mad.

♥

Here we go again.

I was angry and tired. It wasn't going like I'd thought it would. I'd figured if I could just get right with God and confess my sin, He would reward me with a healing process. I had sinned, yes, but I had also obeyed and dealt with the sin honestly—with God and with Mona and with my church.

I had done everything the way I was supposed to, yet the situation just wouldn't get any better. I had expected a rocky road, but I hadn't expected the road to get steeper and more treacherous with time. It seemed the more I tried to smooth things over, the angrier Mona got. Her barrage of questions continued to increase, and my anger reached new depths. I had committed the sin, yes, but how much punishment was I supposed to take?

After a few months, the shock wore off for Mona. I think she honestly wanted to forgive me and keep the marriage going, but as she became convinced of my sincerity, she grew angrier and more demanding. She insisted that I spend every waking moment convincing her I was here for the duration, that I wasn't going to quit.

And I had better answer every question exactly as I had answered that same question the last time—and the time before and the time before. Any slight variance in my answer was cause for suspicion: Why had my answer changed? What wasn't I telling her? What lie had I just been caught in? It was an endless assault.

Is this the life, the wife, I can expect from here on out? Am I never to be more than her whipping boy? It seemed the further we went into the supposed healing process, the further we went from a marriage partnership. I was beginning to lose hope. Quite frankly, if this was the way our lives were going to be, I wasn't interested.

So what's up with this, God? You brought me through for this? You've guided me … here? I've been faithful in every way since my confession. So where are You? Where is Your mighty healing power? I thought You were on my side.

As I sat there screaming this prayer to God, I began to feel guilty. Who was I? The adulterer! The infidel! Who was I to think I deserved anything better? The issues that had brought Mona and me here were becoming more evident to me, and I was beginning to understand why many couples don't survive infidelity. I was questioning our survival for the first time. God's allowance of divorce for adultery was beginning to make sense. The wounds were so deep for both of us. The intense pain pushed me to think about self-preservation and less about "us" preservation. But through all this I knew in my spirit that God wanted us to survive; it was in His will for our marriage to make it.

But where are You, God? Where are You now?

Then I heard His still, quiet voice say, *I'm right here. And, Gary, I'd rather have you right here, angry with Me, than not here with Me at all.*

Those few words spoke volumes to me, that picture of a loving Father wanting His angry son. How gracious He is. My anger didn't push Him away. Our relationship meant more to Him than how I was behaving at the moment or how I had behaved in the past. His was the ultimate example of commitment.

Was it even possible that could work with Mona, too? My anger at God had faded when I heard Him say out of love how much He wanted me with Him. My thoughts recalled the days of sin when I'd felt so far from Him. I'd come back, but anger had surfaced in me when the times got hard. Could that be what Mona was doing too? And could my expressed desire to be with her have the same effect on her anger?

Within a few short moments, a rush of understanding flooded my mind and heart. Suddenly I saw the parallel of my relationship with God in my relationship with Mona. The *agape,* self-sacrificial love that God has for me was the only model I could follow to get us through this crisis. It wasn't going to come from me but from Him through me. The only thing I had to do was to stay committed to God, to Mona, and to our marriage recovery.

Not in my strength, Lord, but in Yours.

THE STORY ON COMMITMENT

So just what is commitment? It is purposed; it is active. In the case of adultery recovery, it is primarily a decision to do everything within your power to heal your marriage. We made mistakes. We both struggled. But we were committed, and eventually with God's help we processed through.

Even more important is to whom and what you commit. Some committed people have created big problems because they were committed to things that did not edify their marriage—like an infidel being more committed to a partner than to his or her spouse, or a spouse being committed to making sure the infidel suffers as much as he or she is. Both are examples of commitments that cause more harm than healing. Equally deceptive and harmful is a commitment to making sure your spouse now becomes the person you always wanted him or her to be.

We encourage you to consider and acknowledge just what it is you are committed to. This is a long and difficult journey. Identifying what you commit to will enable you to make decisions based on that commitment rather than your emotions. You'll face many obstacles, but you can get there. Commitment is one of the major tools you'll need.

Commit to God

The primary commitment that will influence much of your behavior is commitment to God. We each had to commit that we would walk this path with Him. That meant we'd sit at His feet, seek His guidance, and be willing to do it His way. The truth is He provides the strength and the energy for this journey. His guidance is stable when our emotions are in such turmoil. In the midst of the worst times, all we could do was ask Him to guide us, to reveal the next step we should take.

Mona, the fixer by nature, found she needed to wait for the Lord's guidance and refrain from acting on her own. Gary, the conflict avoider, found he needed to act when the Lord did indeed guide him. Both of us found these roles difficult, but our motivation came from our commitment to God. We could do for Him when we had no desire to do for ourselves individually, much less for each other.

We got so weary, feeling like we had done all we could do. We began to ask ourselves if maybe restoring our marriage was just too hard. Then the Lord would remind us that it was indeed too hard for us, but not for Him. He would renew our strength and guide our path. He reminded us of who He was and that nothing was too difficult for Him.

Some days all we could do was cry out to Him, but that was enough. He who created marriage is worthy of our commitment, and we can trust Him. He is faithful.

If this sounds too simplistic, we suggest you sit at His feet in prayer, honestly state your feelings, and ask for His help. Then wait and see what He does.

Commit to Self

Second is a commitment to yourself that from this day forward you will focus on being the husband or wife God has called you to be. Decide that when you don't want to do what you know is right (and there will be plenty of those times) you will admit your feelings honestly to God and to yourself. At times, we had no desire to be godly spouses. We asked God to give us hearts that would honor Him.

The infidel's commitment to be the spouse God has called him or her to be permanently seals the separation between infidel and partner. Ideally, there should be absolutely no contact between them. If that is impossible because of other circumstances, like an unavoidable work situation or a neighbor, we suggest the husband and wife discuss how that contact will be handled and agree together on the boundaries. Any contact should be as brief as possible and impersonal. Affair partners cannot be friends; it just doesn't work, and it will damage the healing process in the marriage. This is a huge issue and needs to be addressed. Some find changing jobs to be an easier alternative than continuing to work near the partner.

When things get tough at home, and they most certainly will, Satan will be right there to tempt you to run back to the partner. Rejection of these desires is imperative and will be a vital part of your recovery. Denial that these desires exist will only increase your vulnerability and risk. Be honest with yourself and with God. Recognize the source of these desires is based on a lie. And the relationship you'd be running to is based in fantasy. Focus on the commitment you've made that is based on truth.

For the spouse, this is an opportunity for prayer—like you need another one! But God calls us to pray for one another and gives us a specific prayer for this circumstance: "Therefore I will block her path with thornbushes; I will wall her in so that she cannot find her way" (Hosea 2:6). Pray that the way of sin would be difficult, that God would surround you and your mate with a hedge of protection.

We often had to battle feelings of "I was a good spouse" or "I could be a much better spouse if he or she would …" or "I have done enough." The reality is that the marriage needs to change. Or maybe how we respond when our spouse comes to us needs to change. Most of us find plenty of issues to deal with that need change. We're not talking about why the adultery happened and we're certainly not addressing fault. We're simply referring to being the husband or wife

God called us to be, and none of us are perfect in that area. The only one you can change is you. It doesn't mean you throw away what was good about you. Keep on doing what was right. It means you commit to evaluate yourself honestly as the spouse God has called you to be.

However, you are not to measure yourself against whatever you think your spouse may have wanted you to be. Gary's partner wore high heels; Mona did not. During the early days of our recovery, we went shoe shopping together and bought a pair of white heels. They were attractive, and Mona wanted to be attractive to her husband, so she put them on. She wore them once; her feet ached within a half an hour. In addition to that, the shoes became a visual reminder of the pitiful truth that she was competing with her husband's partner. She threw them away because they were far removed from what God had called her to be and were in fact a detriment to our recovery.

This is all too common. Of course, it's not shoes for everyone. But the principle and the motivation behind the choice are the same. You are not committing to be the spouse some other person wishes you would be, only to fulfilling God's purpose for you and your marriage.

Commit to Your Spouse

Lastly, commit to your spouse. Commit that you will do everything you can to establish an environment for healing. Commit to being honest from this point forward, which can be a difficult journey for some of us. It means acknowledging that dishonesty led you down your current path. It means admitting to your spouse that a healthy marriage requires trust and intimacy and that you are willing to cultivate those qualities in your relationship. Some people choose infidelity for reasons that have nothing to do with their spouse and more to do with their personal issues. Even if that is the case for you, as a spouse now having this knowledge, you can become an advocate for your husband's or wife's healing.

Committing to your spouse also means deciding that you will not be satisfied with anything less than full healing, no matter how long it takes. None of us ever want to come here again. We tell couples to be more afraid of not healing than of going through the healing process.

Some of you are probably sitting there saying, "Commit to my spouse? This is the person who just took a two-by-four to my marriage and my heart." We understand the emotions. Please note your commitment is not to overlook the past or pretend like nothing happened but to provide the environment for healing, to be willing to work together for something worth saving.

The desire to avoid being injured again is real. For Mona, it took time and many small tests to see if Gary really meant it when he said he was committed to healing. Gary sat through many hours of honest pain, discussion, and sharing of truth. He had to be willing to give Mona time, to endure the tests, and to pass them. And at the same time, he had to be willing to let God lead his spouse on her own journey of change.

Here is where the real commitment comes in: when you get through the beginning of the rebuilding process, when your spouse begins to move forward, when you begin to relax—and God knows you both need to relax—and you can see a glimmer of light at the end of the tunnel. This is where you can make a critical and costly mistake. This is where you can really blow it.

How? Stop working on the marriage. Shut down. Determine you have done enough. Let us reassure you of the truth of the old saying, "It ain't over till it's over." Healing is a process, and in the situation of adultery, a tediously slow process. You each will process at your own pace. Remember, the infidel began this process before the affair even began. The spouse typically begins at revelation. Also, each of you will have separate personal issues in addition to your couple issues. If a healthy marriage is your goal, you must allow your mate to process through in God's time. It is worth it!

Commitment to God, yourself, and your spouse—in that order—enables the process to move forward. We realize that some will struggle with this order. Shouldn't self always be last? Isn't putting self above your mate one of the things that got you here? We are not recommending this for a lifestyle, only to help process through the adultery. Remember, your commitment to self is not for self-satisfaction. It is a commitment, from this day forward, to focus on being the wife or husband God has called you to be. Adultery is a train wreck. Each of you is severely damaged emotionally, spiritually, and physically. Healing that damage takes time.

Your number one commitment to God will remain unchanged. We are confident that as He heals you and your marriage, He will correct as He sees fit. We know that if we had not focused on these three commitments, our marriage most likely would not have survived. We hated why we had to do this, and it was the hardest thing we ever did, but we are so glad we did it.

Questions for Consideration and Conversation

1. Gary and Mona both shared a little about their pasts. Can you identify things from your past that will influence your commitment to the healing process?

2. Share with each other the reasons you are willing to try to heal from adultery.

3. Gary's commitment to healing was tested after a few months. What has caused you to question your commitment?

4. If your spouse were to list what you have done that expresses your commitment to healing, what would they say?

5. Are you committed to doing this God's way? Why or why not?

6. The second commitment was to focus on being the husband or wife God has called you to be. Where do you think you've done well? Where do you think you need to improve?

7. What does an environment for healing look like to you? What part of that do you struggle to provide?

8. Can you commit to being honest? Do you fear your spouse's response?

9. Gary and Mona both encountered a time when they wanted
    to give up because it was too hard. Have you been there?
    What could your spouse do to help you work through those
    feelings?

10. Read Psalm 37:5–6. Do you believe God will help you on
    this journey? Why or why not?

3

Faith

Consequently, faith comes from hearing
the message, and the message is heard
through the word of Christ.

Romans 10:17

GARY'S STORY
(Revelation day)

I wasn't stupid. I knew it was wrong. I knew what the Bible said about adultery. I'd read about hardened hearts and people left to their own perversions. I knew these things. So how could I, a Christian, be buried up to my eyebrows in sin? In adultery? Why couldn't I just stop?

Driving to work that Monday morning, I was again plagued with these same thoughts. Where was God? Why didn't He help me with this? I had been with "her" again last week. Then I'd spent the weekend wracked with guilt and begging God for forgiveness. I had been in that place many times. I knew in my heart of hearts that the only way out was to do something drastic. I needed to cut off the sinful relationship and confess to my wife. God had been telling me that all along. He wouldn't leave me alone about it. But how could I do it? Owning up to my sin would affect not only my marriage but also my entire family, my business, my church, my public ministry. Nothing would be untouched, nothing untainted by my black-hearted behavior.

I hadn't gone looking for this. Neither had she. It had happened slowly—two lonely people, two neglected spouses. A friendship that grew more intimate over time. No matter how I justified it, though, God kept bringing spiritual conviction to my secular lifestyle. Many times the pastor had said in his Sunday sermons, "My door is always open," and I knew God was talking to me. *Oh, God, forgive me. Help me! Give me the strength to stay away from her this time.*

As I pulled up into the office parking lot, the back door opened, and out walked my twenty-year-old engineer. He was an easygoing guy, talented, and doing well in the studio.

When I got out of the car, I noticed the look on his face. He didn't look happy. *Great! Employee problems are all I need. Don't I have enough to deal with? Thanks a lot, God. I pray to You for strength, and just where I need it the most—the office where both she and I work—You turn up the heat.* I felt my heart race as I walked into the office with my engineer. I needed some relief, not more pressure.

His greeting consisted of "We need to talk."

"Okay," I said. "Let's go into the studio." He led the way.

When he pulled the door closed behind him, I knew my instinct had been right. This was not going to be a good day. My anxiety level rose. Was he going to quit?

I could tell by the way he sat that he was nervous and uncomfortable.

"I come to you quoting Matthew 18:15–17. 'If your brother sins ..., go and show him his fault.'"

I knew the passage. "If your brother sins against you, go and show him his fault, just between the two of you. If he listens to you, you have won your brother over. But if he will not listen, take one or two others along, so that 'every matter may be established by the testimony of two or three witnesses.' If he refuses to listen to them, tell it to the church; and if he refuses to listen even to the church, treat him as you would a pagan or a tax collector."

"Gary," he said, "I believe you are in sin. After wrestling with God for a while, I went to my pastor. He advised me to confront you with this. And so I am." He paused, sighing as if he'd just completed a very difficult task.

"What?" I exclaimed. "What makes you think that?"

What did he know? How could he know? She and I were good—as far as lying goes. We knew how to keep our affair discreet. We were careful around everybody, and especially around fellow workers. I couldn't imagine even a hint of suspicion, but if there was suspicion, there was absolutely no proof. *I'll find out what he thinks he knows and just keep lying. I have to, for all our sakes.*

He continued. "I believe last week when you and your coworker went out of town for that meeting, you did more than just meet with clients. I believe you are having an affair."

My mind raced. *What had happened? How could he know? He couldn't. And who is he to confront me? I'm his boss! I'll just deny it.*

He went on. "I believe you need to see your pastor and confess."

Oh, sure, just walk in and ruin my life and the lives of everyone I care about. Does he not comprehend what he's asking? Does he not realize that he's putting his job in jeopardy?

"If you don't do this, I'll be forced to go." He went on to quote the instructions in Matthew.

Slowly but surely, I realized what courage this young man had mustered to be obedient to God. I realized that God was using him to spur me to action. I was tired of lying. I was tired of running. This wasn't the help I'd prayed for, but I knew God was helping me. I took a deep breath, paused, and exhaled. The fight in me melted away; submission to God came. He wasn't going to let me go on. He wasn't going to let me continue in my sin. He was giving me the motivation I needed to get out of this sin.

"Okay," I said. "I'll call my pastor."

And so began the day that would forever change my life.

MONA'S STORY

(Less than six months after revelation)

I don't think I can stand this anymore, my mind screamed. Here I was again, sitting in church with my two younger sons—alone. And there, just a few rows up and on the right, "she" sat. Only she wasn't alone. Her husband was with her, and he had his arm around her. How could I worship when my husband's partner sat in the same church? *Oh, Lord, help me.*

My ears could hear the music. My eyes could see people singing. My mind was beginning to panic. Blood rushed to my head. I could feel palpitations in my chest and such anger and vile hatred in my heart. What was I doing here? What kind of a Christian was I?

Then, as if on cue, my boys started to act up—squirming, talking, playing with whatever was at hand. My quiet reminders went unheeded. They didn't want to be there either. This was a mockery.

How many people knew about the affair? I didn't know and would never know. How I wanted to scream at them all, "But he really loves me!" Why would they believe me? I wasn't sure I even believed it. He didn't even sit in church with me. Both he and she had been removed from all public ministries, but my husband was allowed to continue working in the sound booth behind closed doors. It was a perfect hiding place for him. And it made me angry. I couldn't hide. I couldn't have him with me. I got the kids—unruly and undisciplined. Anyone who was watching was probably thinking, *Well, we know there are problems in* that *family.* I felt as if I were wearing a sign that read "NOT GOOD ENOUGH!" Not a good enough wife, not a good enough mother, not a good enough Christian.

The music continued. We stood. We sat. They prayed. I prayed, *Help me!* More music. Announcements. Time to greet. Stand up, shake hands, and smile like nothing was wrong.

"How are you?"

"Fine."

But there they stood. I could still see the happy couple, shaking hands, smiling. Even when I tried to look away, my eyes were irresistibly drawn to them. How could they keep up this facade of normalcy? How could I?

More music. I couldn't even pretend to sing anymore. I was going crazy. My body surged with adrenaline. I was beginning to cry. *Hide the tears. Don't let the boys see.* "Shhh, be quiet, honey, we're in church."

We sat down. The pastor got up and began to speak. What was he saying? I couldn't hear him. The blood pounded so loudly in my ears I thought everyone around me could hear it too. *I can't do this. I'm going to be sick.* Vomit rose in my throat. My body shook uncontrollably now.

I'm not hiding this well. I'm losing control. I'm going to stand up and scream like some pitiful, crazy wife from a B movie. I have to get out of here. I can't stay here. But what about my boys? Who will stay with them? What will I tell them? They won't know what to think. I'll frighten them. Not to mention how they would distract those around us if I left.

We had decided to stay in this church because of the children. They had gone here all their lives. Their friends were here. And our oldest was struggling spiritually—we didn't want to help him run from God. If I jumped up and ran out of this church, what would happen to my boys? Weren't they going through enough at home? Besides, we, too, had friends here. We, too, had support here. We'd lost so much already. Did we have to lose our church, too?

But I can't stay here! I can't sit here like nothing's wrong when my heart is breaking, when my heart is filled with ugly emotions that override my joy and peace. If I sit here any longer, I'm going to be sick. I'm going to lose what is left of my mind. I am dying. I am broken and bleeding just as surely as if someone shot me with a gun. I'm not going to make it.

And then I felt it. An arm around my shoulders. I heard a whisper in my ear, "You're not alone." I knew without looking there was not another person beside me, yet I could feel that arm around me. Maybe I really was crazy. Maybe I had lost it after all. Or maybe what I claimed to believe in was true. I could feel the calm enter my body. Jesus was there with me in that church. I wasn't crazy. He was real, and He was with me. I could feel His arm around me. I could sense His comforting presence telling me I wasn't alone, I would never be alone. He and I would sit there together with these precious children. He and I would go through this entire experience together.

My body calmed down to a level where survival was an option. I may not have heard the sermon, but I did meet my Lord at church that day. And I went home like I did most Sundays: I hid in my room and cried, because in a very real sense I had lost my church. It would never be the same again. I would never be the same again. The Lord's presence enabled me to get through that day. He would be faithful to get me through many more days. It did not take all the pain away or solve all the difficulties that came from this sin. He did not make it all right. He did what He promised—He comforted. Just as the healing of my marriage would take time, my faith, too, would grow slowly over time.

The Story on Faith

When we think of people of great faith, we think of great people. In our thoughts, we paint the picture of a person whose great faith provided a serene smile and a calm demeanor at all times. Hebrews 11 is often called the "hall of faith," yet if you read the Old Testament passages about the people listed in that chapter, you will find they were just ordinary people who struggled with personal weaknesses and failures in the midst of life's circumstances. What set them apart was that they learned what "living by faith" meant. And that was also what made a difference in our recovery.

Let's define the word *faith* before we go on. It's one of those words that often means different things to different people. The simplest, most accurate definition is that faith is believing what God says to the extent that it influences your thinking *and* your behavior. Faith gives your belief substance and makes it a tangible thing. It is by faith that we act. Hebrews 11 is full of "by faith" this or that was done.

Let's look at God's definition of faith in Hebrews 11:1, "Now faith is being sure of what we hope for and certain of what we do not see."

What we hope for in faith and are certain of is what God has said. We have faith that He is who He says He is and can do what He says He'll do. God is not a vending machine that will give us what we want—even what we think we need—if we'll just insert the right faith coin. Standing before Him and demanding what we think we're due is not faith. The core of our relationship with God is love between Him and us. Faith believes in the reality of that relationship as God describes it in Scripture. That relationship is perfected in our obedience and severely disrupted by our disobedience. Faith means abandoning all trust in one's own resources and implies complete reliance on God and full obedience to Him.[1]

Jesus was the perfect example of that relationship and that obedience. We saw that clearly in the garden of Gethsemane. Jesus knew what was to come. Luke 22:42 says, "Father, if you are willing, take this cup from me; yet not my will, but yours be done."

The often-quoted Romans 8:28 is incomplete without verse 29. Verse 28 says, "And we know that in all things God works for the good of those who love him, who have been called according to his purpose." Then verse 29 continues, "For those God foreknew he also predestined to be conformed to the likeness of his Son, that he might be the firstborn among many brothers." God's purpose is that we would be like Jesus. Nowhere does it say His purpose is to make us healthy, wealthy, and happy. Jesus came as a servant sent here for the salvation of humankind. The point was to provide the bridge so God could have a relationship with us. It's about God. It's not about us. God will use whatever serves His purpose to enhance His relationship with us, to make us more like Jesus, who had the perfect relationship with the Father. Within that relationship, we receive joy and peace, irrespective of our circumstances.

Bearing these truths in mind, we would like to share with you how our faith made the difference in our recovery. And how God helped our faith grow during that process.

Our Faith Grew Because We Found That God Is Enough

We, along with many others with whom we have discussed this issue, have found God sufficient only when He was all we had. Not that He wasn't sufficient before, but we hadn't ever realized it.

Mona grasped this truth one evening after yet another extended time of talking, tears, and pain. As she stood in the doorway between the bedroom and master bath, she suddenly collapsed onto the floor.

"This is killing me, and I really don't think I'm going to make it through." She suddenly realized she had lost not only her marriage and her husband but also part of herself.

There was absolutely nothing left to hang on to. She found herself completely insufficient for the first time in her life, and terror gripped her. That night, God gave Mona the knowledge that she would survive—not that everything would be okay, but that He would enable her to survive. She would be okay whether or not the marriage healed. She wanted the marriage to survive, but if it didn't, she would survive. The peace that came with that realization was tangible and a definite turning point in her recovery.

Also during this time, she came to understand that she had put Gary above God. It was not that she thought Gary was God—especially now—but she looked to Gary to be her source of strength, comfort, and love. What she learned was that Gary would fail in that regard. Mona had failed when Gary had expected her to be the same for him. It was a role God never intended for any human being to perform. We are all incapable of fulfilling it. Life would be easier, better even, with Gary as her husband, but he wasn't necessary for her survival.

We were forced to focus on God because we had nothing and no one else. Even those who loved us and knew what was happening were incapable of fully meeting our needs. This understanding came at great cost, but it is a lesson we wouldn't trade. In understanding this, we received the benefit of an environment conducive to healing and eventually a healthier marriage. We understood Paul's words in 2 Corinthians 12:9, "But he said to me, 'My grace is sufficient for you, for my power is made perfect in weakness.'" The New Living

Translation is even clearer: "Each time he said, 'My grace is all you need. My power works best in weakness.'" Our faith grew because we found we were not enough and God was.

Our Faith Grew Because God Never Left Us

That day in church Mona learned that God had never left her. In the worst of times, aloneness penetrated our souls, but it also provided us with an opportunity to realize God's continuing presence. Can we leave God? You bet. Whenever we turn our backs and disobey, we walk away from Him. But He is always there, waiting for our return. Our relationship with the Lord is the only truly secure relationship we'll ever have. He is the only one capable of being 100 percent faithful 100 percent of the time.

Gary experienced this reality in the midst of his adultery. God chases us and woos us back. He is always there ready, willing, and able to reestablish that relationship He so desires with us. Gary had made the mistake, committed the sin, effectively turning his back. But God chased him throughout it all. Gary would cry out repeatedly to God, "Help me! Help me!" And God would. He would tell Gary the way out was to confess and repent, just as He'd told people from the beginning of time. He used books, sermons, conversations, and any number of things. The answer continued to get clearer in Gary's mind. The conviction of knowing the relationship was a sinful one would not leave. The truth that there was no future for either party in a sinful relationship would not leave. Gary got caught in what he calls the "confession deception." He would fall. He would cry out to God and confess with the intention of never falling again. Then as time went by, he would fall again, and the cycle would repeat. God kept chasing him. The truth of Matthew 5:29–30 became clear: "If your right eye causes you to sin, gouge it out and throw it away. It is better for you to lose one part of your body than for your whole body to be thrown into hell. And if your right hand causes you to sin, cut it off and throw it away. It is better for you to lose one part of your body than for your whole body to go into hell."

The point here is not self-mutilation but rather that sin requires drastic measures. Gary had to do something drastic, or sin would continue to have its hold on his life. He had to separate himself from his partner and demolish the power of temptation and secrecy. God kept telling Gary, *Whatever it takes, do it. Come back to Me; I'm here with open arms.* Only later did we realize the context of Matthew 5:29–30. Jesus was talking about adultery in the preceding two verses.

Becoming aware that God would indeed never leave us or forsake us (Hebrews 13:5) allowed us to experience the reality of His sufficiency. Our faith grew because God never left us.

Our Faith Grew Because We Learned the Truth about God's Comfort

Somewhere we had gotten the idea that if God comforts us, then the pain goes away and the circumstances right themselves. Mona once heard a retreat speaker clarify that false thinking like this: "God promises to comfort us. The problem is we want to be comfortable." The truth of that statement hit solidly home at this point in our lives. Mona was angry with God, impatiently waiting for Him to do His comforting.

When she finally understood the truth—that God comforts us *in* our troubles, not *out* of them—she saw how often He'd been there, comforting her. Like that day at church, like later that day when she finally could pull herself up off the bed, and every single instance when He had used someone or something to help get her through one more hour.

We all want the pain to go away. We want it to be over and let us have our lives back. Sin truly is ugly and pervasive. Fortunately, because of Jesus, God forgives our sin, and we can have a love relationship with Him. Unfortunately, the consequences of our sin remain. Some consequences will be temporary and perhaps not too severe. Other consequences will have a life of their own, and we will be freed from them only at heaven's gates. Through it all, however, we have the promise of God's comfort. "Praise be to the God and Father of our Lord Jesus Christ, the Father of compassion and the God of all comfort, who comforts us in all our troubles" (2 Corinthians 1:3–4). Our faith grew because we learned the truth about God's comfort.

If we had not leaned on God, we would have been tossed about like a rowboat in a hurricane. We have observed other couples in our groups going through similar struggles. None of this is easy. It took everything we had just to keep putting one foot in front of the other each day. There was no magic formula, just absolute and profound truth. Choosing to believe the truth is the foundation of faith. That truth is available to all of us in the Word of God. He is faithful. He is trustworthy. He is the rock our faith can rest on.

Questions for Consideration and Conversation

1. Gary prayed for God to help him out of his sin, but that help was not what he'd expected. What have been your expectations for God's help in this crisis?

2. A speaker Mona heard said, "God promises to comfort us. The problem is we want to be comfortable." Are you willing to be obedient to God if it's not comfortable?

3. Read Hebrews 11. What behaviors of the following individuals enabled them to be listed as part of the "hall of faith": Enoch (Genesis 5:21–24), Abraham (Genesis 12:1–4; 15:6), Rahab (Joshua 2:8–16)?

4. What has been your definition of faith?

5. How is Jesus the perfect example of the relationship God wants with us? See Luke 22:42 and John 6:35–40. Do you believe there is joy and peace in that relationship? Why or why not?

6. Have you put other things or people above God? What did you think they were doing for you?

7. What does 2 Corinthians 12:9 mean to you? Can you share an example of this from your life?

8. Discuss with your spouse where you are in your relationship with God.

9. Do you have more faith in yourself and your abilities or in God?

10. Do you believe you'll be okay with God no matter what your spouse does or doesn't do?

4

Admitting Our Roles

The LORD is near to all who call on
him, to all who call on him in truth.

Psalm 145:18

MONA'S STORY
(Less than one year after revelation)

The intervals between counseling sessions seemed like years to me. Our counselor was busy, and sometimes we had difficulty scheduling as frequently as we wanted. Strangely, I hadn't even wanted to go for counseling in the beginning, but now I couldn't wait to get there. It was the only place we could really talk about what had happened with another person. Our families didn't know, so we had to pretend everything was fine when we were with them. At church, other than the pastor, the deacon board, and a couple of close friends, we didn't know who else knew what was going on in our lives—and we certainly didn't bring it up.

I so often wished there were little flashing neon signs on the foreheads of those who knew. I'm not sure what good it would have done, but I wanted desperately to know who knew about this most intimate part of my life. Who saw me and thought what? Did they think, *Poor Mona. She didn't do anything to deserve this?* Or did they think, *Poor Gary. We saw it coming; she must be so difficult to live with?*

God only knew what they thought of Gary. He said he could tell who knew—especially the women. They treated him differently now, and they didn't want their husbands with him. The fact that Gary's partner walked these same church halls only enriched their imaginations.

No, there was no one we could really talk to—only each other and our counselor.

We needed outside input. Who knew if either one of us even had the capacity to see things clearly anymore. And we needed someone who had some idea of what we were dealing with.

I wanted to do this right. I wanted this to count for something. I did not want to go through this heart-wrenching process and end up with a marriage I wasn't glad we'd saved. The possibility of going through this pain and torment to be just another statistic was more than I could handle. And just how were we to deal with the previous twenty years of marriage? Were they worthless? Was our marriage a sham from day one? I couldn't believe that. We loved each other! We had been happy!

I dragged my thoughts back to the present and focused on today's counseling session. As painful as these times were, at least we worked on the problem. All these months later, I still had difficulty believing we were going through this. I sat there while we got through the pleasantries, thinking, *Come on, let's get on with this; we only have fifty minutes.*

The counselor asked how we were doing. *How are we doing? What does he think? My heart has been ripped from my chest. There's a bleeding, gaping wound that may or may not heal. Gary looks in the mirror and sees a despicable person, a liar, and a cheat. Or at least I think that's what he sees. I look at Gary, and I don't know what I see anymore.*

God, I need a miracle here. You are the great Healer. Heal us! Let me wake up from this nightmare. We're sitting here breathing, and yet as surely as there is air moving in and out of my lungs, I know we're dying. But I want to know why I have to die when the sin is not mine! I didn't do this. Gary did this. She did this. I know I wasn't a perfect wife, but who is? Gary hasn't been a perfect husband, either. Isn't that what marriage is about—loving and respecting in spite of imperfections?

The conversations—both in my head and in the counselor's office—were not going as I wanted. We were discussing everything but the adultery. I remembered that in an earlier session the counselor had suggested a book on codependency. I had almost laughed out loud. My faults lay in control, not in dependency. I had looked at him and asked, "You think I'm codependent?" Calmly he looked directly at me and said, "I know you are."

Well, I'd taken that book home to prove him wrong. But I read it and realized he was probably right. I hadn't known people like me could be called codependent. I always thought codependent people were the ones being controlled, not the ones doing the controlling.

I'd also seen some interesting things about my relationship with my father, how he had urged me to play a role in his life I never should have played. It was nothing sexual, but inappropriate just the same. That was all interesting enough, but that was not why we were here, and I didn't want to digress again. If he handed me another book, I was going to scream!

The counselor grabbed a book from his shelf. Only this time it was a Bible. How could I object to that one? I claimed to be a Christian. I claimed to love this book. But I already knew what God said about adultery. Didn't this guy realize how desperate we were for help?

He opened it and read Ephesians 4:31–32. "Get rid of all bitterness, rage and anger, brawling and slander, along with every form of malice. Be kind and compassionate to one another, forgiving each other, just as in Christ God forgave you."

This wasn't about adultery. It wasn't even about marriage. We were going to get a lesson on forgiveness. Didn't this guy understand the wound of adultery?

He pulled out a tablet and wrote down the words *bitterness, rage, anger, brawling, slander,* and *malice.* He proceeded to define them. My visual of a barroom brawl was replaced by a visual of an angry person, boiling over, yelling, crying, using words that caused injury. Did I really need this? I saw myself way too clearly in what he said, but didn't I have a right to these emotions? Look at what had been done to me!

The counselor went on to talk about repetitive patterns and how people respond to them. He talked about the hurt these behaviors caused. *Wait a minute; we're not talking about just since revelation of the adultery, are we? We're talking about how two people interact. Let's be honest; we're talking about me. We're dissecting Mona as a person, Mona as a wife. Why am I the one being examined and revealed? I haven't committed adultery! Am I not suffering enough? Are you going to beat me down until I'm just a spot on the floor? Until I no longer exist at all?*

He drew two stick figures and wrote the words *critical spirit* between them. He agreed that only the Lord could meet all the needs of another person, yet He instructed us in His Word on how to treat one another. The counselor then went on to define *kindness, compassion,* and *a forgiving spirit.*

The conviction of that drawing, those definitions, was overwhelming. I wasn't a shrew. But I did have a critical spirit. It slipped out sometimes. And maybe I didn't even try to hide it at home. More important, I knew Gary had experienced my critical spirit much too often. He didn't think he was even important to me anymore.

God, please tell me this didn't happen because of how I've treated him. I was just tired. I had three active little boys, one of whom was a challenging child in every situation. I had a demanding, stressful job. Somewhere along the line, I had run out of resources, run out of desire, run out of kindness and compassion for my husband. I had figured Gary loved me enough, knew me well enough, to understand that our time would come later. What was that line from the song? "Life is what happens while you're busy making other plans."

Had Gary's life gone on while I'd planned for the future? Had he taken his "unmet needs" elsewhere? Mona had been a bad wife, so poor Gary had to go to someone else? I felt rage growing inside me.

I felt myself puffing up with indignation. And then suddenly I knew the truth. *Oh, God, I wasn't really that bad, was I? I didn't really cause this, did I?* I don't remember if I actually verbalized the question, but I do remember the answer.

"There will never be a good enough reason for what Gary chose to do. There will never be a good enough reason for the adultery."

The counselor went on to explain that Gary's choosing adultery was his way of dealing with our problems. However, if we really wanted to heal, we would need to identify those problems and deal with them together, in a healthy way.

I resisted. I didn't want to look at and identify our issues as a couple. There was already so much pain in just dealing with the adultery. But I knew if we were going to heal completely, we would have to look at ourselves, at what "we" had become. We had to give each other hope that this journey would be worth it.

God, give me the strength.

GARY'S STORY
(Less than six months after revelation)

"Where is the anger?"

I looked at my Christian counselor, his head cocked to one side, his forehead crinkled, and a very determined, pondering look on his face as he repeated himself. "Where is the anger?"

This was one of my first sessions alone with him. I had just spilled my guts, saying, "How could I have done this to such a perfect wife? How could I have been so selfish?"

But he just kept staring at me and asked again, "Where is the anger?"

What is he talking about? I'm the bad guy here. What in the world did I have to be angry about? I didn't have any right to be angry! I was the liar. The cheat. The adulterer!

I asked him what he meant. He smiled and explained, "I just don't see the anger here. I know it's there. Nobody does what you did without it. You must be angry about something Mona did or didn't do. You aren't being honest with yourself if you deny that she had anything to do with all this."

"Wait a minute!" I said. "This isn't her fault. I'm the one who had the affair."

"Yes, you did," he agreed. "But a relationship is a two-sided thing. If you really want to heal your marriage, you're going to have to stop blaming yourself and start looking at your relationship honestly from top to bottom."

It was about time to wrap up the session. He told me to go home and do some soul-searching. He wanted me to get alone with God and ask Him to reveal to my heart the absolute truth about the relationship Mona and I had.

And so I did. I prayed that God would reveal truth to me. As I prayed, I kept thinking of a time when Mona and I were in the kitchen. I don't remember what we were talking about at the time, but we had the dogs and the kids underfoot as usual. The decibel level was a little too high for my taste, but that's the way it is with three rowdy boys, so I had just learned to live with it.

I remember coming up behind Mona while she was stirring the spaghetti sauce on the stove. As I placed my hands on her hips, I felt her stiffen and pull away. I looked at her, and she was frowning at me. I leaned over to give her a kiss. She leaned slightly toward me, never closing her eyes, and gave me a stiff-necked "grandma" peck on the lips.

"Our time will come later," she said.

Her reaction had pricked my heart. "Okay," I said with a smirk and went back to my seat at the kitchen table. I really hadn't thought much about it until a week later when we were entertaining friends. All the kids were off in the family room playing. The four adults were sitting around the kitchen table, talking and sharing stories about the rigors of raising children. She said it again. "Our time will come later." This time I really heard her, and the words cut me like a knife.

I understood what she meant. She was saying that once the kids were grown, once all the important jobs were done, once everything in life that had real meaning was taken care of, then and only then would there be time for us, for me. I was the low man on the totem pole in her life. I wondered how I had gotten so low on her priority list, and then I just filed the incidents away.

At the time, I had rationalized she couldn't possibly mean it the way I'd heard it. But the more I prayed now, the more those pictures, those words, returned to my mind. "Our time will come later." I had always believed that I was second only to God as a priority in her life. Then came the kids, and after them came everything else. But maybe I was wrong.

I had stuffed the memory of those interactions with her in a dark and hidden place in my heart, where they had festered. I had been angry! I was angry now! How could I have not seen this truth? Could this be one of the reasons I had been vulnerable to adultery? Did I feel so unimportant in my wife's life that I went out and allowed myself to become important to someone else?

The more I thought about it, the more I realized what had been lying under the surface in my mind. Mona had time for everyone else—her kids, her family, her friends, her church, her work, her Bible study, her social life. Everyone and everything but me!

Wait just a minute. If I had really been bothered that much, why didn't I just go to Mona, sit her down, and have a heart-to-heart? I knew the answer to that question. I am the epitome of a conflict avoider. And at this low point in our relationship, we were having enough troubles with our kids, and I felt it was just better to stuff my feelings and concerns way down inside and try to forget about them rather than make things even more uncomfortable by trying to work through them.

I hadn't known how vulnerable I was. I never intended to have an affair. I never thought I would. And then along came a person who listened to me and cared about my problems. She was having problems in her marriage also, so we could help each other. We never had any intention beyond being two caring Christians helping one another along the terrible path of being a neglected spouse. One step followed another and another, and before I realized what was happening, our "friendship" had grown into something more. I was caught up in an affair.

Even as I thought these things through, I knew I had no excuse for my behavior. There is no reason good enough to justify adultery. But perhaps this was one of the reasons I could identify as I began this long, soul-searching, difficult process of what I was to eventually call "peeling the onion"—removing the outer layers of our relationship, trying to comprehend what had happened to us. Trying to heal.

God had started revealing to me the absolute truth I was praying for. Our counselor had been right. I was angry.

The Story on Admitting Our Roles

Whenever we get to this point in our groups, we can see the various reactions on all the faces. We can almost hear the thoughts bouncing off the walls. *Don't even try to tell me this is my fault!* the spouse is thinking. And the infidel asks, "I just destroyed our relationship, and now I'm supposed to sit here and tell my spouse what I don't like about them?"

Both in their own way are saying, "Let's stick to reality and talk about the adultery!" Just like Mona was thinking in the counselor's office.

As we have worked with couples over the years we have found that it's important to understand that there are two areas of adultery recovery.

One is the adultery itself. That was a unilateral choice made by the infidel. Both of you will deal with the consequences that choice brings. Let us again reassure you: There is no reason good enough to justify adultery.

But the second area of recovery deals with the marriage that the husband and wife have had, evaluating what was good and what needs to change. Admitting our roles in the decline of our marriage does not provide "the answer" for why the adultery happened. And in some rare cases the roots of a person's choice to be unfaithful are much deeper and came even before the marriage. But many more of us do benefit from looking at our roles in the marriage. This is an opportunity to evaluate the behaviors, attitudes, and responses that have been allowed to exist in your relationship—some of which were not and still are not conducive to a healthy marriage. Not one of us has been the perfect spouse. Adultery recovery offers us an opportunity to deal with these issues while God has our attention.

Just as surely as God instructs us in His Word how to treat other people, He also tells us how to handle problems with people. Perhaps if we were wiser, we'd focus on the former and have no need for the latter. But we're people, and people make mistakes. People hurt the people closest to them. And if you are reading this, then there likely have been some significant hurts in your marriage. Sometimes the greatest hurts are accomplished by not saying anything or by our reactions when something is said.

When our children were little and one of them suffered a scrape, Mona the nurse would always take him in and wash the cut. This was never a fun time. Washing a scrape hurts. Our son wanted to just leave it alone or at most run water on it. He never wanted his mother to actually touch the thing. Mona would then explain if he wanted it to hurt a lot more, he could leave it alone and let it get infected. The choice was little pain now or big pain later; he could choose.

We have the same option over and over in our marriages: little pain now or big pain later. Many of us choose big pain later, and we often get more hurt than we ever bargained for.

This sounds like spilled milk or sour grapes, you may be thinking. How does looking backward help healing after adultery? Let us offer what we've learned about "cleaning the scrapes" that will help you in your journey toward rebuilding your marriage.

All marriages have issues. You had issues within your marriage before the adultery. You will have issues after the adultery. The difference will be in how and when you handle those issues. Some of the bigger problems we had, such as where Gary ranked on Mona's priority list, needed immediate attention. But some just needed to be discussed and allowed to exist within our relationship. The point is to keep the things that can separate us to a minimum.

For example, sometimes we expect others to do things they are not gifted to do, yet we hold them to the task as if it were the only proof of their love acceptable to us. In our case, Mona wanted Gary to plan surprises. She felt Gary could show her how much he cared by taking the time to do something for her simply because he knew how much it would please her. She wanted him to take care of all the details and do it well. For her birthday, ten months after revelation, we were going to go to the ocean for the weekend. Mona wanted Gary to plan it, and he offered to do so. This would be a new way he could show her love. The end result was both of us sitting on our bed the night before we left, in tears, with no hotel reservations. Everything nice was booked. Gary felt like a jerk who had failed yet again. Mona was disappointed because her preconceived weekend didn't materialize.

In the end we went, we stayed in a so-so place, and we clarified a part of our relationship: Gary is not a planner. He never has been. Mona is. She is detail oriented and thinks things through. Neither Gary's lack of planning nor Mona's ability to plan had anything to do with our love for each other. Therefore, Mona became the official planner for the family. She would not take offense at Gary's lack of planning, and he would not consider her planning a control issue. They would discuss ideas, she'd research and come back for discussion and agreement, and then she would book. It has worked well since.

The point is that not all issues will be resolved the way you may have envisioned. Nevertheless, you need to discuss them. It took some honest conversation and some changes in our thinking for us to understand the other's expectations on the planning issue. You will need to do the same with your issues. And don't worry about whether anyone else has solved the problem the way you do. If your solution works for your relationship and you are both in agreement, stop there.

Trying to discuss relationship issues when you are exhausted, angry, or hurt can be senseless. Plan times and be willing to work on an issue when you're not in the thick of it. And yes, it may not be the most fun you'll have as a couple. But we believe it will facilitate many more fun times in the long run. Think of it as defusing a bomb Satan would love to plant in your home. Obviously, not every issue will be a onetime discussion. It's a marriage-for-a-lifetime plan. And only the two of you can really decide which issues can be allowed to exist within your relationship and which need to be dealt with and eliminated.

Listen to your spouse and make sure you understand what they're saying. Just because you don't agree with their perception of something does not mean they are wrong. Sometimes we don't hear ourselves very well. Mona didn't really comprehend what she was conveying to Gary when she said, "Our time will come later." But what she meant wasn't as important as what Gary heard. What

Gary heard and understood was that he didn't really matter, and that became his reality. Mona felt overwhelmed by her responsibilities at the time and thought that Gary would understand she wanted to pay attention to him when she could really focus on him—without the distraction of family and work. She wasn't making a conscious choice to lower Gary on her priority list. It happened insidiously while she waited for the opportunity to focus on Gary. Mona didn't wake up one day and say, "I don't care about Gary," just as Gary didn't wake up one day and say, "I think I'll have an affair and destroy my life." Both made a choice that in the end proved to be unwise and harmful to their marriage.

It's been said that if Satan can't get you to sin, he'll keep you busy. This is most often the case at home and in our marriages. Indifference is the mortar that can solidify a wall between two people, who one day may come to their senses and face an impenetrable barrier.

You can avoid building walls and eliminate misconception by caring enough to raise issues you find troubling, to honestly express how you see things. Care enough to listen without getting defensive. Care enough to find a way back to each other. You already know what can happen when you try to avoid pain. Be thankful for little pain now. But give your spouse the consideration that communicates, "I value you enough to listen to your perspective even if I don't see it the same way." And then do it. Listen!

We all want to express ourselves. We all want to explain why the situation really isn't as bad as the other person sees it, why we really didn't mean what our spouse thinks we meant. We want to fix the misconception or even deny the wrong. That approach is not likely to solve the problem. If your spouse perceives an event or conversation differently than you do, the perception he or she has is real and requires your respect. However, it doesn't make either of you right or wrong.

When you both understand the problem—when you have heard each other—together you can find a solution that works for both of you. As we learned to listen and give each other respect, there were times Gary would give up something that wasn't as important to him because Mona's viewpoint felt important to her. Sometimes it would be the other way around. Maybe Mona agreed not to take things so personally and to let go of things that weren't that important to her. We both learned to flex where we could. And when we both equally felt that the issue was important, we continued to work at it until a solution was found that we could both live with.

The point is that this is your marriage; the two of you have to live with your decisions, so the situation is not resolved until both of you agree that it is.

Don't Avoid the Issues

Unfortunately, we have had couples in our groups who continue to avoid the issues festering in their relationship. They cling to the anger and pain caused by the infidelity and are unwilling to listen or talk to their spouse about issues. "It'll never change," they say. Sadly, we've had couples go through our groups and deny they even have issues. Yet, after intensive time spent in our group setting, it's easy for us to see some of the issues from the other side of the table. Our hearts grieve, and we pray that God will reveal to them whatever work needs to be done.

Sometimes bad timing gets in the way of couples confronting their issues. Immediately after revelation, emotions are in turmoil and on overload. Hearts are raw and wounded. Looking at roles in the marriage, at issues in the relationship, can come later when you've gotten a little foothold again.

Let us caution you, however. While it can be easy to get comfortable and welcome any semblance of normalcy, don't get caught up in the misconception of thinking you've dealt with the issues. Many times the issues you'll deal with can take a while to come to the surface, and they won't be resolved with one or two conversations. We encourage you not to lose sight of the necessity of confronting them.

One of the most common issues we see is in the area of controlling behaviors. It's a huge issue but can present itself in many different ways. Sometimes we control with anger—if we get mad and loud, the other person gives up. Sometimes we control with a smile and an attitude of graciousness—but we don't change and rarely listen. Sometimes we control by just doing what we want without discussion—then deal with the consequences later.

A marriage is an equal partnership, and if either spouse is feeling controlled, resentment usually results. Be afraid. Be very afraid of what can happen if you do not deal with these issues.

No matter what role you played in the adultery—infidel or spouse—rebuilding your marriage requires you to be honest about the issues. Resist the temptation to avoid addressing the behaviors, attitudes, and responses that have been allowed to exist in your relationship and are not conducive to a healthy marriage. Both of you have the right and an obligation to honestly look at the roles you each played because what you want is a marriage you each enjoy and benefit from. Working through these issues now can pay huge dividends, and perhaps you both have new ears and eyes to assess your contribution.

Unresolved issues will follow you wherever you go.

Trust God to help you find new ways of dealing with old problems. He got you through the revelation; He can get you through the rest.

Finally, don't be afraid to come back to something after you thought it had been dealt with. Revisiting an issue doesn't mean your marriage is on the rocks; it simply means you are now aware and you care about keeping your relationship healthy. You may need clarification on a particular point, or you may just want to check in with each other to see if your solution is still satisfactory to you both.

The fact is neither of us got a lobotomy after the adultery, and some of the things that contributed to our issues were our personalities. We're still the same people, just more willing to work together for the greater good of our relationship.

Your marriage relationship is the most important human relationship you have. It deserves every ounce of energy and love you put into it.

Questions for Consideration and Conversation

1. After reading Mona and Gary's story about admitting their roles, can you see the necessity of this being part of adultery recovery? Why or why not?

2. The counselor said, "There will never be a good enough reason for adultery." Do you believe this is true?

3. Can you separate the adultery and the marriage issues and deal with them individually? Why or why not?

4. Mona just wanted to deal with the issue of the adultery. Why is it a good idea not to limit your recovery to that issue?

5. First Corinthians 7:28 says, "But those who marry will face many troubles in this life." Why do you think that is true?

6. Have you been able to identify an issue in your marriage that needs to be addressed? Does your spouse agree?

7. Is it hard for you to bring up an issue? What could your spouse do to help you?

8. Which frightens you more—dealing with an issue or not dealing with an issue?

9. Is control an issue in your marriage? Can you each describe how you feel when that happens?

10. Read Ephesians 4:2–3. How could you apply this to dealing with issues together?

5

Never Going Back

*I will listen to what God the LORD will
say; he promises peace to his people, his
saints—but let them not return to folly.*

Psalm 85:8

GARY'S STORY

(Less than one year after revelation)

The spa on our deck had become a different place these last few
months. What used to be family time with the kids had turned
into couple time with Mona and me trying to work through the
chaos of our lives. One spa night in particular triggered a turning
point for us.

It had rained earlier that evening, and steam rose slowly from
the water. I felt like a prune because we had been there for well over
an hour, "talking it through" again. I could see that every question
she asked and every answer I offered sent her trudging deeper into

the pit of depression. I was growing more and more concerned about whether or not she was ever going to pull out of it. I knew God was with us, but I didn't know how we were ever going to get past this horrible darkness.

I prayed, *God, what do I do? How do I answer her? Should I be honest? Even if I hurt her?*

God answered me with another question: *Do you want to go back to the way it was?*

No! That was one question I didn't have trouble with. The way our marriage was hadn't been good enough to save us from this. The way it was didn't keep me from drifting away. I absolutely did not want our relationship to go back to the way it had been! If we were going to go through the pain and agony of getting down to the real problems of our relationship, honestly and tearfully asking and answering the hard questions that would bring us to real healing, then I couldn't take the easy way out now. I had taken the easy way by not addressing our problems, and that had brought us to this place. I knew I never wanted to come back here again.

Mona interrupted my prayers and thoughts, asking the one question I had dreaded more than any other, the question that required an answer I knew she would probably not understand. "Will you ever do this again?"

"No, of course not!" should have been my instant answer. But I couldn't say it, so I hesitated. I wanted to be 100 percent honest in all my answers from here on out. I'd never thought I would commit adultery in the first place. How could I really know I wouldn't do it again? I couldn't tell the future. I'd never believed we'd ever have to deal with adultery. I had pledged my faithfulness at our wedding with great sincerity and had not kept that promise. I didn't want to ever again make a promise I could not keep. I tried to explain my hesitation, but it was too late.

She was instantly outraged. She screamed at me, "You *can't* tell me you'll never do it again?"

I kept trying to explain. "I don't know the future. And if I am going to be absolutely honest with you, I can't just say what we both want to hear."

That wasn't good enough. She jumped out of the spa and stormed into the house, crying. After closing up the spa, I finally caught up with her in the bedroom. She was in bed, the lights were off, and the room was completely silent. I tried to talk, but she wouldn't respond. She was shut down, turned inward, and totally engulfed in her own abyss.

I feared what she was thinking. How could I be honest and not cause more pain? After trying again and again to draw her out of her silence, I finally gave up. Maybe time and rest would help.

The morning brings a new day, but not that morning. I woke up next to a woman emotionally detached from me and everyone else. She didn't say a word except what was absolutely necessary to get the kids ready for school. Once they were set, I took them to school and returned home.

I barely got through the door before she said, "We need to go to the counselor now!" I had never seen her like this. She was hard as steel, cold and determined. "You make the appointment, or I will," she said. "In fact, you don't even have to go, but I do."

I tried to talk about last night's unresolved conversation, but she stopped me before I even got out five words.

"Okay, fine. I'll make the appointment myself!" she said.

I assured her I did want to go with her, and so I called. I told the counselor's delightfully cheery receptionist we needed an appointment today, and I wasn't kidding. "It's today or perhaps never again." On hold I went, and within seconds she was back. "We've had a cancellation. Ten o'clock okay?"

"Perfect," I replied, and I thanked God for providing.

Ten o'clock was only a couple of hours away, but it seemed like an eternity. I resisted the urge to turn on the radio to drown out the silence on the trip to the office. I think we were in the waiting room only about thirty seconds before the door opened and our counselor stepped out, smiling. He took one look at Mona and his expression dropped.

Once behind the closed door of his office, Mona didn't wait for any formalities. "He can't say he won't do it again! I can't do this anymore. I don't think we're going to make it. I think we have to separate." Then she broke. "Why can't he tell me he won't do it again?" Tears streamed down her face. "Why?"

The counselor directed his attention to me. "Gary, are you planning to commit adultery again?"

I replied without any hesitation, "No, of course not!"

"Then why can't you tell her you won't do it again?"

I began to explain. "I am not going back to the way it was. I am not going to tell Mona what I think she wants to hear or not tell her something I want to say, just to avoid dealing with her reaction. I am only going to tell Mona the absolute truth. I can't predict the future, so therefore I can't say with absolute honesty I will never do it again. I thought I'd never do it in the first place."

I watched our counselor relax just a bit. Then without missing a beat, he repeated his question, "Are you planning on doing this again?"

"No, of course not!" I said emphatically.

He then turned to Mona. "Can you hear what Gary is saying?" I watched as her troubled and overwhelmed mind tried to assimilate what was happening. I saw a sense of understanding begin to dawn across her face.

Oh, Mona, please understand. I'm not saying I can't tell you I'll never do it again because I want to give myself permission. I only want to be completely honest with you and with myself. I don't want to break another promise to you ever again. I want to someday be able to talk with you honestly and not see pain envelop you. I want us to survive. I can't go back to who I was; therefore, we can never go back to who we were.

MONA'S STORY

(Less than one year after revelation)

"I will not go through this again! Do you hear me? I will never, ever go through this again!"

The high-pitched, passionate, and loud voice I heard was my own. I was furious, and screaming at my husband seemed to be the only way to let him know how I felt. Gary looked so very weary, and our three young sons were in a nearby room, undoubtedly terrified and unsure of how to respond to my tirade.

What had happened to our family? What was happening to me? I stormed down the hall to my room and closed the door, once again effectively ruining any chance of a "normal" evening.

Since the night Gary had told me about his adultery, time had rearranged itself. It was all divided into "before the affair," "during the affair," and "after the affair." I didn't know which time was the worst.

Before was a sham, a fraud I had perpetuated. Had he ever loved me? What else had been a lie?

During was nothing but being lied to and being so very stupid. How many times and in how many ways had I implied or even outright commented on what a good marriage we had to my "friend," his partner?

After was hell. Plain and simple. Pain, every day, all day. I was incapable of being a good mother, a good friend, a good anything. Anytime there was a moment's release from it, I made sure it didn't last long.

In my weary brain there were only three alternatives: lying to myself, being lied to, or pain. If there was no pain, then someone must be lying. At least the pain was real. In one of her books, author Barbara Johnson wrote about a home for the bewildered. That was where I needed to go. My tears had far outnumbered my smiles for a very long time.

How long had it been like this? I could tell you exactly how long it had been since that night Gary had walked into our bedroom and confessed his affair of three years with my best Christian friend. What I didn't know was how much longer the pain would go on. How much more could our family take?

Gary was ready for peace; he needed it. Well, too bad. My peace was gone too. But what about my boys? Didn't they deserve some time without turmoil? Was I to live a lie for my children's sake? It was all so intense. I couldn't figure anything out anymore. I couldn't even take care of my children. I was going nuts. If Gary's adultery didn't destroy us, it looked like my craziness would.

I'd been off work today and needed to get some cleaning done. Life does go on and dirt still accumulates even when you're falling apart.

After getting the kids off to school, I began my housework. I started in the bathrooms. Three boys made the bathrooms a priority.

One bathroom done. As I gathered up my cleaning supplies, I once again felt the weariness creeping in. I was so tired. I wondered how Gary did at work. Was he tired? Or was he able to focus on work and let all the emotional stuff go? How I wish I could.

Then it happened again. I "saw" them together. Gary and his partner. One scene after another. Conversations I imagined they'd had. Touches I imagined they'd shared.

Stop it. Stop it. You can't go there.

I sat on the bed and allowed the thoughts their freedom. Were they meeting? Had they talked? Did he miss her?

My tears flowed and pain wracked my chest.

After some time, I shook my head furiously and jumped up from the bed. *No. No. No! I will not do this! I will not be consumed with this!*

I knew God wanted my marriage to heal. I knew Gary and I both wanted to heal. I also knew who didn't want us to heal. Satan's attack on my mind was clear. But I was so tired of fighting.

By the time Gary got home, dinner was ready and the kids were hungry. We sat down together at the table, and conversation flowed back and forth.

Everything seemed so normal. Descriptions of a newly built Lego structure by our oldest son. A brief report on activities of the day. A bit of acting up by our two younger sons. A request for that night's story. Could they watch a particular TV show? Don't talk with your mouth full. Sit down and eat. What was the best thing about school today? I watched it all as if it were happening to some-one else. A father and his sons, eating and talking. Smiling, laughing. I was getting nauseous.

After dinner, the boys went off to do chores and get ready for bed. Gary and I cleared the table together, as was our habit. He paused and looked at me, asking if I was okay. Did he think for a minute I could be okay? He said he didn't know how to help me anymore. I said I couldn't pretend we were okay. We weren't. And if I started pretending, then we would be living a lie again. And then at some later date he could again walk into my bedroom and destroy the family, destroy whatever was left of me. Then I declared I couldn't go through this again.

So here I was. Behind the closed door of my bedroom in agony, listening to my family, listening to the sounds of people I couldn't feel further from if we were separated by an ocean.

God, help me! I just can't go back to the life we had. It had been a lie that I thought was true! There was more to this than just Gary's adultery and our marriage. There was also me. Who was I? Who would I become? How could we—I—possibly slide back into being a happy little Christian family? And yet what was the alternative? Constant upheaval? Endless pain? *God, it feels so very hopeless. Help me to find my way!*

THE STORY ON NEVER GOING BACK

We were extreme in our reactions to "not going back." It took time to work all those labile emotions into a healthy resolve of not going back to what hadn't worked for us in the first place.

Mona had to deal with the issue of what to do with the "before" part of the marriage. Was it worthless? Had it indeed been a farce? What was she to do with our years of marriage before the affair?

And Gary had to deal with the issue of his dishonesty—his ability to lie convincingly, something neither of us realized he could do.

And both of us had to deal with our ability to lie to ourselves and to discount warning signs.

So what do we mean by "never going back"? Clearly, neither one of us knew what that meant in the beginning. Adultery recovery is overwhelming, all-consuming. It is a rare person indeed who can think clearly in these circumstances. The one clear thought we both had was that we were not going to waste the opportunity to truly heal our relationship. We both fervently agreed that we would not smooth this road over until the foundation itself was firmly set. The "never go back" principles that follow helped us rebuild the underpinnings of our marriage, and we trust they will help you, too.

Never Go Back to Believing You Cannot Fall

The first thing we determined was that we would never again think either one of us was above falling into adultery. Our smug belief that we had a marriage that was impenetrable by an outsider was permanently removed. What we came to understand was that no marriage is beyond penetration. The self-assurance that this is one area we could never fall into is a lie for every couple who believe it. Godly people sin. Godly people fall. Good marriages have problems.

Adultery is an equal opportunity sin. It transcends social standing, intelligence, age, race, religion, and spiritual maturity. Many of us don't want to believe that, especially about spiritual maturity. But think about the spiritual leaders who have fallen.

The truth is that all people can fall. Given the right circumstances and the right person and the right opportunity, anyone can commit adultery. In fact, Dave Carder has written a book detailing just how that can happen. In *Close Calls! What Adulterers Want You to Know About Protecting Your Marriage* he describes how easily that can and does happen.

If that is true, then what can you do to be less susceptible? First and most important, you pray. Ask God to reveal truth about your marriage that you may be missing and be willing to take the time and energy to address problems before they gather strength. Next, we believe you become more aware of the "right" circumstances as you keep your eyes and ears open and heed warnings that God is faithful to give us. We each have different areas of weakness. You become more aware of the "right" person as you evaluate behaviors and attitudes expressed by yourself, your spouse, and others. Sometimes "no" is just the right answer. And you become acutely aware of the "right" opportunities and never, ever allow them again. As Paul said in 1 Corinthians 10:23, "'Everything is permissible'—but not everything is beneficial. 'Everything is permissible'—but not everything is constructive." We'll talk more about this when we talk about hedges in chapter 11.

We also believe that once a marriage has been through an adulterous relationship, whether it be sexual or emotional, both parties in that relationship are more susceptible to fall the next time. We are not saying you will, just that you are more susceptible to the temptation. Your oneness has already been broken by another, and Satan can and will twist the truth, tempting you to think that since the damage has already been done, it's permanent. Those thoughts will come at an opportune time, perhaps when you're feeling lonely and isolated or when you're just vulnerable and suddenly find yourself appreciated and cared for by another person. The point is, never go back to believing that you or anyone else is invulnerable to adultery.

Never Go Back to Old Habits

Second, we decided we would never go back to the old habits that helped us make this trip. We would develop new, healthier habits in our marriage. For example, we began to make time for each other, just to have fun together. We also set aside times to have deeper conversations about the future, our dreams and hopes for us as a couple and for our family.

Before that though, we had to identify our negative habits and eliminate them from our relationship. One habit in particular was extremely destructive. Whenever Gary felt like Mona didn't want him sexually, he would withdraw emotionally in an attempt to "give her space and an opportunity to want him." Mona would perceive his withdrawal as his not wanting her and would then withdraw herself "until he wanted her again." Of course, as time went on, we both would end up feeling increasingly unwanted by the other and hurt because of it. Every word and action seemed to underscore this belief.

Fortunately, we were able to act like adults long enough to discover what we were doing. We were in fact able to laugh at ourselves and discover new and effective ways to communicate what we were feeling and what we each wanted. And we will never again consider feeling unwanted as childish or selfish. We will not go back to that old habit.

It will take some time and energy to identify the well-worn paths in your marriage. Often the key is one partner feeling distanced from the other. When you begin to feel that way, take the initiative to talk with your spouse to see if he or she might be feeling the same way. Ask yourselves what words or actions brought on the feelings. Have you felt this way before? Were the circumstances similar? Now's the time to discover the dynamics that have possibly created a destructive pattern in your relationship.

Once you've identified an unhealthy pattern, determine how you will counteract it. You can start by rejecting whatever works its way between you. Do you need to give up an evening out with friends or a church committee or a sports team to communicate to your spouse that he or she is the most important person on earth? Then do it!

Quit saying, "If he or she will do this, I'll do that." Standing back to back with your arms folded and refusing to move will get you nowhere. It's your responsibility to do what you know is right regardless of what your spouse is or is not doing.

Some couples, having discovered a bad habit, have found new ways to communicate and spend time together. Some cook together, take a class together, walk together, or schedule a regular date. There are endless resources out there with thousands of ideas. The point is to identify what you need to change and then work together to make the changes.

Never Go Back to Complaining

Last, we have given up on complaining—especially the most destructive form of all: nonverbal complaining. Silent complaining is what you do when you make a mental note every time your spouse drops dirty clothes on the floor, doesn't brush his or her teeth, doesn't make the bed, doesn't clean the kitchen, doesn't put gas in the car—you name it. If you insist on keeping track of those pesky, irritating behaviors in your spouse, your heart will soon be filled with resentment.

You may think you're being a good Christian—practically a martyr, really—for putting up with all those things, especially since you're not complaining out loud. After all, Proverbs 21:9 says, "Better to live on a corner of the roof than share a house with a quarrelsome wife." And you certainly don't want to be considered "quarrelsome," as a wife *or* husband.

If you continually complain nonverbally, however, resentment will build and eventually spill out. And we tend to express resentment in ways unrelated to the original source, causing divisiveness in the same way verbal complaining does. For example, working late every evening is not the solution to your wife's talking during your favorite TV show. Likewise, slamming pans on the stove is not going to convince your husband that he needs to pick up his dirty socks! If what is bothering you is an issue, treat it as such and deal with it constructively.

If it is simply an annoyance and not worth dealing with as an issue, let it go. We all put up with some things in each other. We'll stop that in heaven, not here on earth. A marriage is not good because you're both perfect. Rather, a marriage is good because you both encourage each other to be the best man or woman God intends. Let's focus our energies on the important things.

Not going back can be hard. We will always want to take the path of least resistance. It is so much easier when things begin to feel normal again. But remember, your old "normal" way of doing things got you where you are. You will have to sacrifice some easy times to create a new normal. Perhaps you'll even find yourselves having to give more than you get in return. We remind ourselves that nothing will ever compare to the difficulty of dealing with the adultery. And nothing will compare with the blessings of a healthy marriage.

Questions for Consideration and Conversation

1. Gary hesitated to emphatically deny he'd ever again be unfaithful because he wanted to be 100 percent honest. Discuss with your spouse what 100 percent honesty is.

2. The "normal" sounds of an evening sent Mona into a tirade. What was it that frightened her? Can you relate to her fear?

3. Has your marriage been divided into *before, during,* and *after* the affair? Discuss this with your spouse.

4. "Given the right circumstances and the right person and the right opportunity, anyone can commit adultery." Do you agree with this statement? Why or why not?

5. Read Jeremiah 17:9. What do you think God is trying to convey to us?

6. Have you identified any negative old habits in your marriage? Does your spouse agree?

7. Do you think you and your spouse have stood back to back waiting for the other to make the first move? How did that affect your healing process?

8. Do you participate in nonverbal complaining? Discuss an example.

9. How might you differentiate between something that is an issue and needs to be resolved and something that is annoying but can be allowed to exist in your marriage?

10. Read 1 Corinthians 10:23–24. Discuss how this might apply to your marriage.

6

Willing to Endure the Pain

Why is my pain unending and my
wound grievous and incurable? …
Therefore this is what the LORD says:
"If you repent, I will restore you."

Jeremiah 15:18–19

MONA'S STORY
(Less than one year after revelation)

I stopped and looked into the living room. My three sons were absorbed in the late afternoon's cartoons. Even my teenager still enjoyed them. I didn't care. There was nothing left in me to care with. I had no energy to guide them into a more productive activity. And the mere thought of trying to convince them to join me in something else was overwhelming. I wasn't a mother anymore. I wasn't a wife. I wasn't even sure there was anything left of the person I had once been. So I didn't say anything.

I simply opened the front door and left. I had no idea where I was going or what I was doing. I just had to leave.

I turned west and walked down our road. We live on a thorough-fare between two towns, and it's always busy, especially at that time of day. I imagined the people in their cars looking forward to being reunited with their families as they drove home. Looking forward to eating a warm meal and enjoying each other's company. I, on the other hand, walked down the road away from everything, feeling only the coolness of the fall evening. Not caring about dinner, my husband, or my children. I was totally numb.

How much pain could one person take before giving up trying to survive? How much time do you get to grieve before you're classi-fied as emotionally disturbed? I feared I was perilously close. And I was angry! Gary and his partner had "repented and been forgiven." They could move on with their lives. Well, I couldn't! I resented the fact that I had not committed this sin, yet I still had to carry the pain. Why didn't they just run away together? By now, I could have been moving on with my life instead of being stuck. And at least I wouldn't have had to suffer in silence; everyone would know if they'd run off. Even as I thought these things, I knew the absurdity of them. We all had suffered. We all were still suffering.

But it was so unfair. No one had ever even wanted to have an affair with me! There had been no desire so strong that I had risked everything to satisfy it. Gary had risked everything and everyone for her. What had he ever risked to have me? Maybe I just wasn't worth having. Maybe I should just disappear.

I found myself at our small community cemetery. I walked around a bit and wondered what traumas were represented here.

Had any survived betrayal? I thought of my father, who had died a few years before, and again felt the pain of his loss. I sat on a rock and cried out my heart to my daddy and my Lord. It somehow seemed appropriate.

The tears ceased eventually. I didn't want to go home and wade through the muck that this healing process had turned out to be. Every time it seemed we were getting closer to being done (whatever that meant), something else would happen. I had never been so depressed. I had never experienced pain of this magnitude, and I didn't want to anymore. I didn't know if I could.

I contemplated not going home at all. How long would it be until they'd miss me? What would they do? No one knew where I was. No one even knew when I'd left. If I were ever going to be suicidal, it would have been now. But something kept me on this side of that ledge. Maybe it was seeing the pain my father had caused our family by his inability to cope with life. Maybe it was just a "God thing."

The hardness and pointed edges of the rock I was sitting on penetrated my thoughts as well as my body. It was beginning to look like rain. It was time to go. But if I went home, I would be walking back into the same house I'd left. I knew the pain that awaited me there. I knew the work that awaited both Gary and me. And I knew the only hope was to walk through this pain—me, Gary, and the Lord.

So I got up from my rock, said good-bye to my dad, and walked home with my Lord.

GARY'S STORY

(Less than six months after revelation)

Our anniversary was coming up. We had been married nineteen years. What made this one a real milestone was the fact that it was just four months after the revelation of my affair. Four long and very painful months had gone by, and we had survived them. Mona was starting to have days without crying. They were few and far between, but we were healing, and that was important. Maybe we were through the worst of it.

I wanted to do something nice for our anniversary, but something expensive and crazy was just out of the question. Neither of us was really in the mood for celebrating.

We talked about it and decided we would go camping, just the two of us. We both enjoyed camping. We camped as a family for vacations. This time we would leave the kids with grandparents and enjoy a few days of peace and quiet. She and I would pull our little home-away-from-home high into the Sierras and get away from it all. She needed a break and so did I.

The campsite went together nicely. Our site was slightly isolated, surrounded by pine trees, just the way both of us liked it. The campground was practically empty. The month of May is pretty cold in the High Sierras, and the weather can be unpredictable, so most people wait until later in the season.

We barbequed some steaks and had a pleasant and relaxed dinner. No interruptions, no spills, no fights. We did the dishes together while listening to the radio, singing to the oldies. The outside air had a definite chill, so we stayed inside the trailer, turned on the heater, and settled in with our books. The quiet, peaceful atmosphere was soothing in the familiar comfort of our little self-contained trailer.

Well, one thing led to another, and pretty soon, there we were acting like twenty-year-olds again. Ironically enough, our sex life had actually improved since revelation. I would learn later that this was not uncommon. But at that point I really didn't understand why; I was just glad something drew us together. At least until Mona began to cry—again. Unfortunately, this was not an uncommon occurrence either. Something triggered something, and a wave of thoughts and emotions seemed to overtake her. What would normally have been an occasion for quiet pillow talk had turned into yet another episode of my holding her while she wept.

I asked what was bothering her. Was it anything I had done or said? "No, it's nothing you did. I just can't help it."

"Is there anything I can do to help you?" I asked.

"No, just hold me."

I held her for quite a while. I was trying to be strong for her. I was trying to hold it all together for us, for our marriage, and for our family.

We talked about what it was that made her cry. For the first time she told me that sometimes pictures of my partner and me would flash through her head while we were making love, and she would just lose it. She assured me it was nothing I did.

What did she mean, nothing I did? How could she even say that? Of course it was something I did. I cheated on her! I allowed another person to come between us. The man she loved without condition betrayed her. I think I had always suspected what it was that made her cry, but I'd never asked before, and right then I was sorry I had.

I had told myself all through the affair that it had nothing to do with Mona, that it was something separate from our marriage, but in fact it had everything to do with her. It could not be separated, and she would bear the brunt of my sin. She felt the betrayal more deeply than I had ever imagined possible. She was lying there engulfed in pain of my making.

And then she began apologizing to me for ruining our time together.

The realization of what my choices had cost overwhelmed me. I lost it. I broke in a new and different way as I comprehended the depth of her injury.

That night I wailed as I began to understand the pain I had caused. I had cut her to her very soul. I had not known I was capable of inflicting such a wound. How could I live with this knowledge? How could she ever forgive me? I honestly didn't know how I would have reacted if the situation had been reversed. How could I even ask it of her to forgive me? What kind of a man was I?

She held me and whispered it was going to be all right. She comforted me while I began to grasp what I had done. I lay there, overcome by the magnitude of the task I had placed before us.

Forgiveness and restoration took on new meaning for me that night.

The Story on Enduring the Pain

Focus on the Family had a radio show in 1983 titled *Victims of Affairs*. Dr. James Dobson related a story that had been told to him.

A woman grew up in the Soviet Union. In 1941, although she was not a Jew, she was put in a Nazi concentration camp until the war was over. While there she witnessed horrific beatings and killings, lost family members, and endured atrocities most of us will never know or understand. She somehow survived, came to the United States, and married. Her husband had an affair and left her for another woman. She had this to say about her experience with her husband: "That was the most painful experience of my life."

When we heard this story in the early stages of our recovery, we wept with relief. We were not crazy or overreacting. We were indeed experiencing the worst trauma of our lives. And it affirmed for us that there could be something even more difficult than what we were going through—to experience this without our spouse.

Adultery causes pain. Adultery recovery is painful. Life becomes a roller-coaster ride. You feel as if you have climbed that first and highest hill, dangled over the edge until you think you'll burst from the suspense, and then you are propelled downward at a stomach-clenching rate of speed. All the while, you realize you have no power to control the fall. The pain accompanies you along this path, the highs and the lows. And just when you think you've reached the end of the ride, a whole new segment becomes visible. And unlike the roller-coaster ride, there is very little thrill to the process.

Most of us fully understand those who say they would give all they have to get off this ride. It affects you physically, emotionally, and spiritually. A weariness previously unknown saps you of your strength. In this circumstance, we can come to understand Paul's words in 2 Corinthians 12:9, "But he said to me, 'My grace is sufficient for you, for my power is made perfect in weakness.'"

If there were only one thing we could say to you who are on this ride, it would be to ride it out. Complete the journey. To jump off in the middle of the ride may feel better now, but in the long run you will find yourself on another ride just as terrifying and painful.

Couples begin our support groups from many different places. Some walk in holding hands, while others seem to keep as much space between them as possible. Some appear strong and resilient; others are so fragile you wonder how they even made it to the group. The one common denominator is the pain. It is expressed differently, it is responded to differently, but it is always present. We tell them that this group is not going to be fun. We tell them this is work—hard and painful work. We tell them in all likelihood they will get worse before they get better. But we tell them it is worth it and they can do it.

Understand the Sources of Pain

As much as the presentation of pain may vary, the sources do not. We have found that identifying the source of the pain is one step toward walking through it.

The Infidel

One primary source of the pain—the infidel's deceptive betrayal—seems as though it would be fairly easy to identify, yet often this is not the case. Gary's excruciating realization of the depth of damage and pain his infidelity caused came only after several months of work and many different experiences. Through our groups we've come to realize that Gary's experience is not uncommon.

It is definitely a healing moment, however, when *both* infidel and spouse can acknowledge the depth of pain the adultery has caused: when the spouse can say they believe the infidel "gets it." Yet that realization is not something that can be forced. It occurs when two people share their feelings in an honest and ongoing process.

Some people attempt to detour around this recognition and find their healing process hindered. One woman told us that her husband's inability or unwillingness to look at his part caused them years of pain.

The Spouse

The spouse needs to realize he or she can contribute to the pain in many ways as well. One of the most common is whom they tell about the adultery and how they share that information. In their agitated, emotional state, spouses often confront both young and adult children, as well as friends and other family members, with facts and information they will later regret sharing. This commonly happens in the early stages after revelation.

The truth is that those who are told all the details about the infidelity are rarely told all the details about the restoration process as it progresses. Yet we expect those same people to follow us on our path toward healing with only half the information. It is an unfairly placed burden on those who love us and want to protect us from harm.

In our case, our children were young, and we did not tell them specifics until we began writing this book. They knew we had problems and knew we were seeing a counselor, but they were also reassured that we were going to try to work it out. Any questions they had were answered honestly and age appropriately. Our responses didn't eliminate the pain for them, but we didn't have to do repair work later.

If you've read the preceding paragraphs with a sinking feeling, please know that it is never too late to set proper boundaries with those who have been told too much. We suggest you go as a couple and explain that you will be working together to heal your marriage. Encourage them to support both of you in a marriage crisis, not just one individual. If you need to apologize for words or an attitude, do so.

We can both contribute to the pain by sabotaging the process if we refuse to be honest or focus on blaming the other. Honesty to a healing process is as vital as a hammer is to nails. Neither penetrates very deeply without the tool. And most of us have plenty of blame to go around. If our focus is making sure our husband or wife hurts as badly as we do, then a lot of energy is being used to incur pain, not work through it.

Early in our groups, we tell the couples that there are no bad guys or good guys here. There are marriages in trouble. And our role is to help the marriages survive and thrive. We encourage them to keep that same focus.

The Culture

Another source of pain is the world's view of marriage and sexuality. Our society is obsessed with sexual relationships. They pervade our newspapers, magazines, television, movies, and even radio. Common conversation between people is littered with sexual innuendo and jokes about sexual behavior and adultery. In the aftermath of revelation, the mere volume of it astonished us. How had we not comprehended the prevalence of this type of conversation? In His Word, God warns us repeatedly about keeping ourselves occupied with what is lovely and pure. We haven't done this, especially as a society. Add to that the fact that in the entertainment industry the infidel is often portrayed as the "good" character, the spouse as one deserving of the betrayal; and the pain quotient goes up.

Don't allow our culture's view on adultery to deplete your resources or keep you otherwise occupied. Working through recovery is worth it and offers much more personal satisfaction. We spent a lot of time and energy beating ourselves up rather than working on our marriage relationship.

End Pain in Healthy Ways

Owing to the fact that this is such a painful experience, we look for ways to escape. Much like the lancing of a boil, the touch required to drain it causes some pain, and the normal response is to pull away. It is easy to fall into thinking that if we'll just leave it alone, it will heal on its own. It feels as though what we're doing is making it worse. In the chapter on talking (chapter 8), we'll discuss more specific principles and tools. However, here we'd like to address two of the most common unhealthy attempts to end the pain.

Spare Me

First is the infidel's desire to spare the spouse more pain by omitting truth or not initiating discussions. A common example of this occurs when the infidel accidentally sees or is contacted by a former partner. The infidel withholds this information from the spouse, knowing it will hurt the spouse and precipitate another long episode of grief.

Unfortunately, we have seen what happens when the information comes out later—and rest assured it will. The spouse feels he or she has once again been deceived and has great difficulty believing the infidel didn't initiate the contact or respond inappropriately to the contact. The healing process in the marriage is set back because the spouse wonders what else they haven't been told.

It is so much easier to deal with truth. And when truth is handled correctly, the infidel has some control over how the spouse is exposed to it.

Acknowledging a contact will indeed bring questions. Don't sidestep them. Be bold. Many episodes of adultery happen within the workplace, so unless the infidel or the partner has changed jobs, contacts will inevitably occur. It is best if your spouse hears this information from you. And if your spouse asks how the contact made you feel, be honest. Most spouses are not opting to stay with infidels who are devoid of emotions; therefore, an answer that denies emotions feels like a lie—again. A simple "I felt sad," "I was very uncomfortable," or "I felt guilty for just being there" followed by an affirmation that this marriage is where the infidel will be putting energy and effort reaffirms the commitment to the spouse.

The point is that one of the biggest hurts experienced by the spouse is the deception. Anything that even remotely resembles deception causes more pain. And we have heard countless times from many, many spouses that they can perceive when truth is being with-held. They may not be able to discern exactly what is or is not going on, but they know something is up.

Short-Circuit

The second common dynamic we have seen is the attempt to short-circuit the healing process by not listening, thus escaping the pain. For example, let's say it's evening. Things feel almost normal at home for a change, and then the spouse brings "it" up again. Or something comes on television about adultery. You want to avoid what you know will occur if this conversation takes place, so you sabotage it by using anger, avoidance, or anything that will create a diversion. In essence you shut your spouse down. The message to the one who wants to talk is to "get over it and move on with life." Even worse is the message, "I don't care how you feel."

This is common to the infidel, but we have also seen it with the spouse. Some spouses are more than willing to avoid any conflict. It seems they are more afraid of the truth than of the illusion of healing. They may feel better momentarily, but their relief will be short-lived, and healing will not be accomplished.

Sometimes we short-circuit the healing process even while trying to look as though we're not. A husband or wife who sits quietly in a chair while their mate explains something can appear willing. But if that person in the chair won't look at their mate—or if they check their watch, cell phone, or task list and appear disinterested—not much healing is happening.

The other consequence of continual short-circuiting is that the spouse loses hope of change. This happens when we feel that we're not being listened to and we begin to believe there is no hope of our input affecting the outcome. Our attempts to communicate, to convey our thoughts, fall on "deaf ears" and we give up. Adultery recovery requires perseverance, and when we feel as though we're not making any impact, our motivation rapidly dwindles.

The truth is that an infidel's desire to "spare" the spouse pain often is more about trying to spare themselves pain. Trying to short-circuit pain usually has the opposite effect as it often results in avoiding or minimizing another's feelings and concerns—neither of which is conducive to healing.

So what do we suggest for those of us who find ourselves surrounded by a sea of pain? Accept it. Pain is part of this process. Don't try to hide it or undermine its presence. Pain can force us to our knees, and that's not a bad place to be if you're a believer. Be willing to endure the pain. Just as physical pain indicates something is wrong and needs fixing, so too does this pain. The pain will begin to ease as we begin to heal.

In Hebrew there is a saying: *Do not prolong the suffering beyond the time of pain.* Enduring the pain is the best way to walk through it. Together you can leave it behind.

Questions for Consideration and Conversation

1. Consider some of the emotions Mona experienced that day on her walk. What are the common causes of pain in adultery recovery?

2. Gary's realization of the pain his adultery had caused Mona was a significant moment in their recovery. Why do you think that is true? What do you think is meant by the infidel's "getting it"?

3. The woman on the Focus radio program said her husband's leaving her for another woman was the most painful experience of her life. Why do you think that is true?

4. Mona and Gary compared adultery recovery to a roller-coaster ride. Can you relate? Why or why not?

5. If you are the infidel, how do you think you have made the pain worse? What are you doing that you believe helps your spouse deal with their pain?

6. If you are the spouse, how do you think you have made the pain worse? What are you doing that you believe helps your spouse deal with their pain?

7. Is there anyone you believe you shared too much with? What do you think you could do to help all of you deal with this?

8. "Spare me" omits truth. "Short-circuit" omits listening. Which do you think you've done?

9. Read Psalm 69:29. Do you believe God directly helps us through times of suffering?

10. Can you share your pain with your spouse? Why or why not?

7

Acknowledging the Losses

There is a time for everything, and
a season for every activity under
heaven ... a time to search and
a time to give up, a time to keep
and a time to throw away.

Ecclesiastes 3:1, 6

GARY'S STORY
(Less than six months after revelation)

The senior pastor set me up with an accountability partner, which made sense, of course. Put the infidel with another person of the same gender to build a relationship, share intimate details of their lives, and ask all the hard questions. The motive was an honorable one, a biblical one.

So we met together on a regular basis. He was already a friend and about the same age. We'd worked together on various projects at the church. He was a deacon and spiritually mature. He'd sit across the table and look at me, pause, and then ask, "Are you really living a godly life?" This man is a wonderful Christian, a servant of our God. I was blessed by his availability and willingness to help. But he really had no idea what it was like to be where I was, and he was in uncharted territory. And because he knew all the parties involved, even his world had been rocked.

I desperately wanted someone who had been where I was and could offer me hope—hope that I could live a godly life. Hope that Mona and I could survive adultery.

What Mona and I were experiencing offered very little hope. She was in self-destruct mode. I was doing everything possible to hold the family together and keep my sanity. But I was flying blind. I'd never been in this place either.

I had so many questions, but my accountability partner didn't have the answers. I could sense how uncomfortable this friend was with me now, but I didn't know what to do. Would anyone ever be comfortable with me again?

It had become increasingly obvious to me that there was a barrier between me and many members of my church family: less eye contact, quick turns in the hallway. I was being avoided. I didn't blame them, though. I wanted to avoid me too. I was difficult to be around. I was the infidel.

I've heard a saying that Christians are the only ones who shoot their wounded. I never would have believed that before, but I sure understand it now. It's not that they didn't care. Most just didn't know how to deal with this issue of adultery. Since I had gone to my senior pastor and confessed, the situation had gone before the deacon board. I had been removed from all public ministry and was under discipline. Mona and I were never told who was aware of our circumstances, but I could tell when I met up with people.

One Sunday after church I was really feeling low about how people were avoiding me, and I told Mona. She offered wisdom when she said, "You are going to have to reintroduce yourself to them. They don't know how to act around you, so they'll avoid you until you initiate contact. They need to be assured that you are the same person you were and that you intend to deal with this sin biblically."

So I went along and tried to "reintroduce myself." That sometimes worked with the men, but it never worked with the women. After analyzing this, I developed a theory of my own.

The husbands don't want to be around me because I make their wives nervous.

The wives don't want me around their husbands because it scares them, as if what I did could rub off on the men. At the least I'm a bad influence.

The wives don't want me around any women and certainly don't want to be seen with me because of what I did to Mona. They are angry with me for causing such pain.

The husbands don't want me around their wives because they don't trust me.

There you have it. No one wanted to be around me. Where do you go for support when the body of Christ runs from you? I didn't know. But I knew I was losing something valuable just as surely as I had lost Mona's trust. I didn't know how to deal with it. I didn't have the strength to deal with it.

Soon my accountability partner and I quit meeting.

To preserve at least a small connection to the church, I spent the better part of that year hiding in the television broadcast booth. I'm a sound and video technician, and they needed my services. They justified allowing me to stay there by saying it wasn't a public ministry. The bonus to me was that I didn't have to face anyone. I could get to church early and go home late.

Not only had I lost my standing in the church; it felt like I had lost my church, too.

Mona's Story
(Less than one year after revelation)

It is such an ordinary chore: standing in my kitchen, cleaning up after breakfast, loading the dishwasher, and looking out my window. My window looks out across our street and into a field. All in all, it is a pleasant and serene view.

That morning, however, my gaze was pulled to the left of our driveway even though I didn't want to look and be reminded. Such an impersonal object, the garbage can that draws my eyes. Such a normal sight. A driveway. Rocks. A garbage can sitting to the left.

Normal. Impersonal. Those words are no longer in my vocabulary. Nothing is normal and everything is personal. I don't know how to live anymore, to function day to day. How do you live when you're not sure there is life anymore?

Last night had started out to be such an ordinary evening. Dinner. Kids. Of course, Gary's adultery and our pain were there—that never went away—but it seemed that maybe we could find a way through this if we could just work hard enough.

Then we'd gone to bed, and the talking began. We had discussed his affair ad nauseam. Every question I asked only elicited an answer I'd already heard, and so I broached a new subject: his one-night stand.

I had felt sorry for her. I always knew she was a pawn in the drama of revealing Gary's sin. She was the only nonbeliever. What an example we had been! She was young, naive. I knew she wasn't innocent, but I held the rest of us as believers in Christ to a higher standard.

I had briefly met with this young woman after revelation. It had, of course, been awkward, but there had been some things that needed to be said. They had been, and that had been the end of it.

I hadn't asked a lot of questions about that night. What more did I want to know? She knew I was out of town with the kids. She knew Gary would be home alone. She had even told him she was coming over. And she had. He'd let her in. They both knew why she was there. She made her intentions very clear. According to Gary, he protested—albeit briefly and ineffectively.

"What did you say? What did she say?" And the tears came again. The pain returned. "Why did you …?" "Why didn't …?" "Where were you?" He told me they had come into our bedroom.

I made some caustic, disgusting remark about that and then suddenly realized where I was. I was in the same bedroom. I was sitting on the same bed, on the same bedspread. Adrenaline rushed through my body. Tears flowed freely. Everything slipped away, and all I could see was my beautiful bedspread.

Suddenly I heard myself scream, and I scrambled off the bed as if it were on fire. I couldn't have been more repulsed if it had suddenly turned into a pile of writhing maggots. I was nauseous. Gary stood, a concerned and puzzled look on his face. He was unable even to speak.

But I was speaking. I was speaking for all of us. I reached out and grabbed at the loathsome bedspread. I pulled and screamed. "Get it out of here! Get it out of here!" I was shaking, crying hysterically.

Gary stooped to pick up the bedspread. So many emotions crossed his face. I think he was afraid to leave me, but he was more afraid not to remove the focus of my hysteria. He walked out of the room carrying the bedspread, leaving me to cower in the corner like an abused child. He returned empty-handed and after some time was able to convince me to get into bed. We once again cried ourselves to sleep.

How could that have happened only last night?

I could no longer keep my eyes from fixating on that garbage can. Our bedspread was in it, and our bedroom was devoid of a bedspread. It had been a convicting visual when I'd made the bed that morning. Something missing. Something so obvious, surely everyone would notice. I had been certain even our young sons would say something about it. Of course, they didn't.

Most of what we had lost because of this sin I couldn't roll up and hysterically demand it be removed from my presence. If I did begin to remove the things that had been touched, where would it end? I'd have to remove my car, my house, our business, my church—the list would go on and on.

Some rare moment of sanity had convinced me early on not to try to remove everything that had been touched by this sin. Not to start a journey that could never be completed. Staring at the garbage can today, I realized the value of identifying what we had lost. And the fact that we would need to mourn those losses. Maybe then we could heal.

Maybe then I could go shopping for a new bedspread.

THE STORY ON ACKNOWLEDGING YOUR LOSSES

The Bible tells us in Romans 6:23, "For the wages of sin is death." Adultery is sin. Adultery involves loss. Adultery brings death. But when you read the rest of that verse, you find hope: "… but the gift of God is eternal life." The point is that in spite of our sin—sin that deserves death—God offers us new life. The same is true for those recovering from adultery. God can and does provide new life for a healed marriage.

There is indeed painful loss for all involved after infidelity. We encourage you to determine what is a permanent loss—like the bedspread. We caution you to make sure that whatever you "throw away" does not contain something you need for life—like trust in a marriage. Some things can be rebuilt even though they were lost for a time.

We neither have to mourn forever nor lose forever. We can move on. We can find new things to laugh about. We can regain something of value.

But we found that not recognizing the loss, not mourning, only made it worse. And we have seen that in others also.

It took us a while to identify the things we had lost, and even when we did, accepting that they were really gone was more difficult than we expected it would be. However, once we were able to name them, it seemed we had taken another step on the path of healing. We didn't feel so stuck. And we began to work through what we had truly lost and what we needed to find again.

As we've dealt with the couples in our groups, we've been able to identify five common areas of loss after adultery. We trust that naming them will offer you hope as well as enable you to move beyond them.

Loss of the Purity of the Marriage Bed

Loss of the purity of the marriage bed may seem obvious, but believe it or not, many people miss it. It wasn't until the night of the bedspread that Mona fully realized the impact of that one-night stand.

We did not become believers until after we'd been married several years. We had both lived worldly lives prior to our marriage. In the first week after revelation, Mona was walking by herself and talking to God. She remembers being struck with the realization that the way she felt about the intruder Gary had allowed to mar the purity of their marriage bed could be how God felt about the behaviors Mona had allowed to mar her purity before she was married. She grieved for the first time, truly grieved her own sin and disobedience, and began to realize that impurities come in many shapes and forms.

God reserves the marriage bed for a husband and wife only. Sex is the one unique aspect reserved for the two of them. It is a picture of the intimate relationship God Himself wants with us as individuals, and the desire represents His intense desire for our hearts. But just as God creates new life in old sinners, He can also create a new and pure marriage bed after adultery.

The effect of adultery on the sexual relationship between a husband and wife following the revelation of an affair runs the gamut. Some experience a renewed vigor and desire for intimacy. Some are so estranged they wonder if they will be husband and wife in that way again. Whatever the initial effect, it does tend to be temporary. There is not, in our opinion, a "normal" response. The effect adultery has on your physical relationship is as individual as your marriage. We believe the physical relationship will reflect the marriage relationship overall. As you work through your issues—*if* you work through your issues—this question of sexual intimacy within your marriage can be resolved. If there were unresolved sexual issues prior to the adultery, those issues will need to be dealt with in a more intentional manner after the adultery. Fortunately, the church has begun to recognize the need for help in this area, and there are ministries with specific helps for couples.

Acknowledging the violation of your marriage bed is horribly painful. We found out from our experience and that of the couples in our groups that tears during intimate moments are common. The tears are there because the adultery raided this area of your intimacy. We encourage couples to acknowledge the wounds. And follow that with reminding each other that even though the injury is real, so too is your desire to heal your marriage. This can be a priceless opportunity for the infidel to reaffirm the choice of their marriage partner and not their affair partner. This is a deep and raw wound, but it is not fatal and can be healed by God.

When your spouse needs to grieve, grieve with them. Acknowledge the violation, grieve the loss, and allow God's healing to progress on His timetable and not yours.

When your spouse needs time, grant it. Some recommend the bottom line be to respect the feelings of whomever is not yet ready for sexually intimate activity and to find out what kind of touch or affection the reluctant or uninterested partner would be willing to accept.[1]

When you need help, seek it. A healthy marriage will include sexual intimacy along with the many different facets of intimacy and marital love. Just as in every aspect of this healing process, be honest with one another, validate each other's responses, and reassure your spouse that you will be there to walk through this pain together. Because the goal is a healthy marriage.

Loss of Faithfulness

For a lot longer than we'd like to admit, we both cringed whenever we heard the word *faithful*. It's amazing how often it is used! Descriptions of good people often include the word *faithful*. But suddenly that word no longer applied to Gary. And that hurt both of us.

Then we looked at the definitions. In the Old Testament, the words translated *faithful* mean "to support, to stand firm."[2] In the New Testament, the words translated *faithful* mean "to be certain, worthy to be believed."[3] The dictionary states that it means "to be true in the performance of duty, vows, or the like."[4] In truth, Gary had failed to live up to these definitions. In truth, Mona had also failed to live up to these definitions, just in different areas.

Faithfulness is to be a lifestyle for every husband and wife, and physical adultery is certainly not the only indication that it is lacking.

Faithfulness can also be lost when there is an emotional affair—even when the infidel's relationship with another has not included sexual intimacies. We'll discuss this more in depth in the chapter on emotional affairs, but suffice for now to say that an emotional affair is also unfaithfulness.

The good news is that faithfulness can be restored. It can also become a new way of life, and that is no less valuable even if faithfulness was not part of a previous lifestyle. We had to mourn the time of Gary's unfaithfulness, but that did not mean his faithfulness to Mona or to God could not be resumed.

Now when we hear the word *faithful,* we feel a twinge. But we will not allow Satan to rob either of us of all the past or future years we were and will be faithful to one another.

Loss of Trust

Trust is lost after the revelation of an affair—not only trust a spouse had in the infidel, but also the trust both had in themselves. The infidel trusted himself or herself to make right choices. The spouse trusted himself or herself to know if bad choices were made.

We'll explain more in depth what rebuilding trust looks like in the chapter on trust. What we need to understand is that, although lost for a time, trust can be rebuilt.

What worked well for us was Gary's willingness to be accountable for all things. Mona didn't have to check on him; he initiated the contact and checked in. He avoided all situations that could have even a hint of deception, and thus Mona didn't feel a need to monitor everything he did.

Dr. Donald Harvey gives the best illustration of what is involved in rebuilding trust that we have heard.[5] He compares the process of rebuilding trust with that of healing a broken leg. There is nothing normal about having a broken leg. It hurts and definitely limits your mobility. But what do you do when you have a broken leg? You put that broken leg in a cast. Now there is nothing normal about walking around with a cast—it's clumsy and awkward and limiting. A person moves from one abnormal situation (the broken leg) to another abnormal situation (the cast). You don't put on a cast to be normal. You put on a cast to get to be normal later.

The adultery correlates to the broken leg. Rebuilding trust correlates to the time of wearing a cast. The things you will both do as you are rebuilding trust will not be normal. They will be clumsy and awkward and limiting—and in the case of adultery recovery they will also be scary. Scary because you know neither of you can live this way for the rest of your lives. The transparency and accountability of the infidel needed by the spouse will be abnormal for a time. But as both of you heal, like in the case of the broken leg, when healing is nearly complete, the cast will come off. Your walk will again be awkward for a while until the healing is complete—then one day you will notice that your walk feels normal for the first time in a long while.

If during this abnormal time both of you focus on rebuilding the trust—being honest about what does and what doesn't help that process—you'll make progress. Yes, trust is lost after the revelation of infidelity. Grieve the time in which it was lost. Then move forward and rebuild it.

Loss of the Belief of Who You Both Are

Husbands and wives are often shattered after revelation because they believed they knew their spouses so well that the person could never have pulled off having an affair. Mona didn't believe Gary *could* lie, and she didn't believe she *could* be deceived.

The reality was that Gary could lie. In fact, he did it very well. And Mona could be deceived—her perception or intuition wasn't that great after all. What does that mean for the future? It means that Gary is capable of lying. When and if he chooses to, he can pull it off.

Infidels are often astounded by their own ability to lead a dual life, to separate one life from the other. Even they didn't think they were capable of it. Yet the Bible says clearly that we are *all* capable of such deceit: "The heart is deceitful above all things and beyond cure. Who can understand it?" (Jeremiah 17:9). Most of us think we are better than that, and perhaps that's the greatest lie of all.

All of us acknowledge intellectually that our lives can be changed in an instant—by a car driven a wrong way, by an illness, or by any number of things. Once a catastrophic event has actually happened, our understanding goes beyond the intellectual into the experiential. Most of us, however, don't quit living. We simply live with the knowledge that bad things can happen, and we try not to do anything to allow them to happen again.

The same is true of adultery. It was always a possibility. You just didn't know it. But now you do. What you've lost is your innocence.

That does not have to ruin your life. It can make you appreciate the good parts of life even more. And it can make you wiser.

Those of us who have been through adultery have seen sides of each other a lot of couples will never know. Not seeing some of those things can be a blessing. Some of what we learned about each other is also a blessing. Mona clearly understands now that Gary is just a man—a man she loves very much, but still just a man. And she is just a woman. Both have value and both prefer to walk this life together helping each other be the best they can be.

Loss of Church

Most couples in our groups lost their churches. The reality is that the church is made up of people. And people are overwhelmed by the fact that anyone commits adultery, much less those professing to be Christians. And the truth is that those involved in adultery recovery do need to regroup and deal with the issues at hand. Church life cannot, nor should it, go on undisturbed.

We were unusual in that we stayed at our church. We simply never felt God direct us to leave. Our children were established there, and it is big enough that many people did not know our circumstances. This is not the norm, and some even advocate moving to another church, especially if the partner is in the church. However, we believe staying was the best decision for us. We would have missed multiple blessings that came from our church family.

Before the blessings, however, came two heavy losses related to our church.

First was the loss of ministry. Gary was often used on the platform for his musical and vocal talents, and occasionally Mona would serve alongside him. Both of us were beginning to be more involved in leadership within our church body. After revelation, we both had to draw back from church involvement—Gary as a result of discipline and Mona because she was barely able to function.

It was a loss that caused sadness, but we do advocate the voluntary resigning of any church leadership position or area of public ministry. It is time to focus on you and the Lord, you and your spouse. Your ministry is now your marriage, and it requires 100 percent of you. People who ask questions can be given a truthful answer without details, something such as, "I need to pull back and focus on my family for a while."

If your livelihood is derived from ministry, obviously there are more issues to deal with. We don't presume to know the answers, but we have all seen many examples of infidelities being hidden and ministries damaged later.

Does that mean you can't ever again serve in any capacity? We believe the leader you serve under should be made aware of your circumstances and should determine the process of restoring you (or not) to leadership. But we are firmly convinced that our service to the body of Christ does not end because of adultery. Each one of us is a restored sinner.

The other significant loss was that of relationships within our church body. Those relationships that were mature and healthy between believers survived. Those that were the Sunday morning "How are you?" often did not. We were not ostracized or condemned to sit in the back pew, but we've had to invest a lot of time and energy to get back to a deep level with some.

We had to recognize that they, too, really had no idea how to handle this situation. And we've had to put forth some effort and allow some time for that broken trust to heal. Some of our relationships were rebuilt. And some relationships developed anew after the infidelity. We cherish both.

Those who were unwilling to process with us were lost. To this day, some people still hold Gary at arm's length, unwilling to experience our former free flow of laughter and fellowship. The truth is they don't want to.

But another truth is that God does want a deep relationship with us, and He will guide us in our church relationships as well as in our marriage.

♥

Acknowledging the losses from adultery is painful. None of us wants to lose anything that is important to us. But only by acknowledging them can we accept them and move forward on our journey toward healing.

Questions for Consideration and Conversation

1. Gary felt he'd lost his church in many ways. How might you react to someone like Gary in your church?

2. Mona permanently lost the bedspread because of what happened. Is there anything you can identify as a permanent loss? Is it something you can live without?

3. How has the infidelity affected your sexual intimacy? Is it something you can talk about together?

4. Do you believe faithfulness can be restored in a marriage damaged by infidelity? Why or why not?

5. Reread the broken-leg analogy on rebuilding trust. What might be some of the things you need to put in place that would represent the cast during your healing process?

6. How has the infidelity changed the way you think about yourself?

7. Have you lost something at your church because of the infidelity? Can you identify it?

8. Read Psalm 46:1–2. Can you identify any way that God has been your help during this time?

9. Which area of loss has affected you the most? Which area do you think has affected your spouse the most?

10. Read Habakkuk 3:17–19. Habakkuk faced terrible loss yet was able to pen these words. Can you believe that God will keep you secure on this journey?

8

Talk, Talk, and Talk Again

Do not be afraid. These are
the things you are to do: Speak
the truth to each other....
Zechariah 8:15–16

MONA'S STORY
(About one year after revelation)

It took so much to act like a normal human being. Performing the everyday activities of a woman and mother required reaching into the deep recesses of myself and dragging up whatever little bit of strength and fortitude I could find. By the time dinner and dishes were done, homework was completed, and the kids were settled in their rooms for the night, I was exhausted.

This healing process had gone on longer than I'd expected. But I couldn't pretend to be healed if I wasn't. I knew Gary was ready to be done with it. Too bad! This trip hadn't been my idea in the first place.

I did have to give Gary credit, though. He was repentant. He made himself an open book and gave me permission to ask any question. He answered a lot of questions I know he didn't want to. Certainly he tried to avoid some—especially about his feelings and thoughts. But he soon realized that if we couldn't come together now, freely and openly sharing, there was little hope we ever would.

Many people asked how I could even consider staying with him. What a question! I'm a Christian. I know what the Scriptures say about marriage. I believe God permitted divorce for the protection of the innocent, but it is never what He wanted. God hates divorce. He said so. And we had three boys. We'd had way too many opportunities to see what divorce does to the children. There was no pretending they'd be better off. But the bottom line was that Gary wanted our marriage to survive. He was willing to go through the hard work of rebuilding. How could I justify refusing even to try?

Gary came out from reading the boys a story. He'd aged a bit. I had too. He looked tired. I did too.

He looked at me and said, "What do you want to do?"

Poor guy. He knew what he was inviting: another talk, more agonizing, more crying. But it seemed to be all we could do. The catharsis never seemed to end.

"Let's go sit in the spa," I said. "It's such a nice night."

So we changed, grabbed a soda, and went out. The night was clear and the sky filled with stars.

We'd gotten the spa and had a gazebo built when our youngest was just a baby. It had been the first "frivolous" thing we'd ever done. But we never regretted it. Our little ones learned to swim in it, and we spent countless hours here as a family—with nothing to do but talk! I smiled as I recalled the laughter and splashing three little boys could cause in this thing. I could look over and see the pool we later added and remember times in the winter when the boys had challenged each other to jump into the cold water. I could see their little bodies running (against the rules!) toward the pool and jumping in. They'd come up screeching after hitting the frigid water. But they'd stay there and swim awhile, then eventually come back shivering to the spa to get warm. Gary and I grinned at each other as we acknowledged how nuts our kids truly were.

But that had changed after Gary's revelation; there wasn't much laughter around here anymore. And if by chance we were able to take a break and enjoy a brief period of family time, one of the boys would act up. Satan had been having a heyday in our home.

We sat in silence for a bit, listening to the water bubble.

"How was your day?" I asked.

We went on to discuss a small problem with a client. We talked about a note we'd received from one of the boys' teachers. It almost felt like a normal conversation for a while.

Then we were quiet again. *Now what?* I wondered. I could feel the emotions coming. The pain. The sadness. The tears brimming in my eyes. I heard my voice asking the questions, heard Gary answering the same questions—again. It was almost as if I were off in a corner, watching two people on a path they didn't want to be on, yet having no idea how to get off. I knew the next question before I heard it. I knew the answer before he said it. There was no satisfaction here, no new information to be had. I searched for a way to elicit new information, trying to figure out what I needed to know now.

And then a thought crossed my mind. *I don't care.* But it wasn't the *I don't care because there's nothing left in me to care with* thought. This was the plain *I don't care to know any more* thought—because I'd heard it all before. Because I was bored!

I was bored with the subject of his affair! I took a quick emotional inventory. Pain? Slight, but not consuming. Sadness? Not really. Tears? Gone. This was weird. Inside me was something I hadn't felt in such a long time. What was it? Disinterest. I simply wasn't interested anymore.

Oh, my precious Lord! What did this mean? I couldn't imagine I would ever feel this way. Would it last? I didn't care!

I interrupted him. "Gary, can we talk about something else?"

Gary's Story
(Less than six months after revelation)

We were in the spa once again, where we could be alone and talk openly without fear of the boys being within earshot and could sit without distractions for a while. So that's what we did, turning into prunes while talking about the affair. I hated it.

I wanted to move forward, not look backward. I didn't want to remember my sin. I didn't want Mona to be able to visualize my sin with such clarity. Talking about it, hearing the words come out of my mouth, caused her such pain. And it caused me pain too.

I lost count of how many times she had asked the same questions. And I was getting frustrated. I knew I didn't have any right to get mad. It was my fault we were here in the first place. But it's hard to answer a question that you know is going to blow your wife's whole world apart. Here you are trying to rebuild the marriage, and with your complete honesty, you seem to be causing more and more pain, going backward with every talk session. You know that after you answer a question for the umpteenth time, she'll be depressed and start crying. Then when she finally starts to show signs of progress, *she'll ask the same question again!* It seemed like a sick process that repeated itself over and over.

Trying to avoid the negative cycle, I would shift into damage control mode. If we could just avoid talking, we could avoid the pain, and maybe we could get back to some sort of normalcy. Wrong! According to her, that meant I wasn't willing to work on our marriage. Therefore, I must not want to stay with her. And then she would get even more depressed.

What were we to do with this? I felt trapped and scared. I knew if I answered with all the details, she would go into another tailspin, and it might be days before she would be able to function again. But if I kept anything back or my answer changed in any way, she would focus on that, and the tailspin would come anyway. Plus, in her mind I would be lying again, and that would set us back even more. There was no way for me to win.

Mona started into a frenzy of questions. The answers felt like both masochism and sadism. What good was this? Mona justified her questions by saying that I had stolen from her and that she needed to know what had been taken.

It was time for me to answer a question. I looked her directly in the eyes and said, "Do you really want me to answer that question?" That stopped her. At least long enough to think about what she was truly asking. I don't remember how I came up with this answer, but it seemed to help. It gave us both a chance to pause and take a breath.

I didn't know how to describe her these days. She was consumed— consumed with pain, consumed with questions. Some days she barely functioned. Other times, however briefly, I could see the rational, confident woman I had married. This question, "Do you really want me to answer that question?" seemed occasionally to speak to that woman.

I could see her mind working, pondering the question I'd asked and the question she'd asked also. I never knew how she would respond. Sometimes, she would look at me and say, "You're right. I don't really need to go there again." Other times, she'd pause, think awhile, and then look at me and say, "Yes. I want the answer. I asked you because I want and need to know."

I didn't really like giving her that power. But I had to agree that she had the right to determine what she did and did not want to hear. I hadn't asked her before bringing this sin into our home. If she was going to live with the consequences of it, then she had the right to determine what she needed to know. If we had any chance of rebuilding this marriage, there was no more room for lies or half-truths.

THE STORY ON TALKING

In our groups, we answer more questions related to talking during adultery recovery than any other subject. We might have thought trust or forgiveness or even sex would come up most often, but in reality, conversation is the bridge that can deliver trust, forgiveness, *and* sex.

We also must say here that professional Christian counseling is a benefit the couple in adultery recovery cannot afford to do without. If someone you love fell out of a tree and was lying on the ground, broken and bleeding, you would get help immediately. Right now, your marriage is lying in the dirt, broken and bleeding. You need help. Once you're established with godly counsel, the three of you can decide how often and how long you need to meet.

What follows is not an exhaustive study of conversation. There are plenty of books devoted to communication styles and skills. We will, however, offer solutions to the most common problems we've encountered both in our groups and in our own recovery.

Avoid Avoidance

So many couples will do anything to avoid talking—and with good reason. Intense emotions, such as anger and fear, quickly boil to the surface and often spill out, making conversations exhausting and painful.

Most commonly, it is the infidel who wishes they didn't have to talk about the sin anymore, feeling the pain and shame of repeated emotional exposure and condemnation. The conversations usually end with the spouse being devastated, depressed, and wounded, so what's the point of talking about it *again?*

On the other hand, we have occasionally seen a spouse who didn't want to talk. The spouse rationalized by saying that forgiveness is enough. Better to let sleeping dogs lie, so to speak. And the infidel was glad to comply, to "spare the spouse pain." On the surface this appears to be a noble gesture.

We are constantly asked about what is best for healing when it comes to asking and answering questions. Most therapists do agree that complete disclosure is necessary for healing. The differences come in defining "complete disclosure" and how long it's healthy for these conversations to continue.

The fear is that too much information can create painful mental images that can haunt and torture. But one of the spouses in a group said it best: "Do you really think the truth can hurt any more than what I'm imagining?" Spouses often report being inundated with graphic images prior to hearing any details. We believe knowing what happened actually can decrease those thoughts and images.

In our opinion the final decision of how much information is shared lies in the hands of the spouse. Dr. Shirley Glass states the betrayed spouse's need to know is the determining factor for how much detail and discussion is necessary.[1] And we agree with Dave Carder that it's a fine line to walk, but better to err on the side of too much disclosure than too little.[2]

If the spouse declines to ask questions, that, too, is their choice. However, the spouse should have the freedom to ask questions if the need arises later—and assurance that the infidel will provide honest answers.

How Long Is Long Enough?

Some spouses have reported that a time limit had been placed on the freedom to ask questions. For example, the question-and-answer conversation was limited to a single session in the counselor's office or a week or two at home. The problem with that is that the spouse often has difficulty processing in the beginning and doesn't even necessarily know what questions to ask yet. On the other hand, if time limits are not set, the fear is that the spouse will "obsess" and healing will be delayed. We encourage you to consider two questions if obsessing is a concern:

Do you really need to know more information?

Do you already know the answer?

We believe the questions will stop as the healing progresses and the spouse becomes more and more convinced the infidel is being truthful. If they're not stopping, maybe there is a healing problem or the spouse believes the infidel is continuing to withhold information. Certainly this is where godly counsel can help a couple make the best decisions for their recovery. When spouses are told the time for questions is over or when information is being withheld, they say it feels like more deception and effectively shuts down the healing process.

To pull ourselves out of the cycle of talking, pain, more talking, then more pain, we used the tool Gary described in his story earlier in this chapter. He would ask Mona, "Do you really want to know the answer to that?" If we were going to rebuild the relationship, Gary needed to provide Mona the opportunity to decide for herself what she did and did not want to hear, in addition to how many times she wanted to hear it. Remember, it's not over until both of you say it's over!

Dealing with Anger

Unresolved anger becomes resentment. Resentment has been defined as "anger with a history," a mutation of a natural human emotion.[3] It's important to understand that anger is a natural response to inflicted or perceived harm.

Our friends Joe and Michelle Williams say that anger is an emotion given to us by God for a purpose. They now consider the emotion of anger as a warning signal for their marriage. To ignore it would be like ignoring physical pain that informs you something is wrong with your body.[4]

Gary had been angry with Mona for a long time before the affair, but he didn't want to upset the status quo by talking about it. And the truth was that Mona wasn't very approachable—he didn't feel safe bringing his concerns to her. We were both, in hindsight, aware of his resentment developing, but neither one of us took the initiative or expended the energy to deal with it. His unspoken resentment unnerved Mona and created an atmosphere conducive to an affair. How we wish now we had dealt with the issue of his anger!

There are a couple of principles that can help you deal with unresolved anger. Don't allow your anger to control you. If we are out of control verbally or physically, we are in sin. And the truth is that no real work gets done in that atmosphere.

This is a time when it is appropriate to call a time-out. Each party should have permission to say "I cannot talk about this right now. We need to come back to it later. Let's talk again in an hour" (or whatever time frame seems most appropriate). Indeed, this will probably not be met with great enthusiasm, but it needs to be allowed. Our greatest caution for those choosing this option is to make sure you keep your word and come back to it. And that responsibility falls to the one who called the time-out.

Additionally, it is important to understand that processing and venting are two different things. Processing implies movement and change. Venting implies release, getting it all out. Processing frequently involves venting, but the end result of processing is to let it go.

We need to be willing to let the anger go when we've dealt with the cause. It feels so good and so right, especially if you're the one who's been wronged. And we believe some hold on to their anger because it feels better than the pain that can often follow. There are some answers that will never be sufficient for understanding what has happened just as there is no reason that justifies the choice of adultery. Be willing to talk about the causes of your anger so you can deal with those and the emotion can be let go.

Keep It Private

Find private times for these discussions. As we've told you, many of our discussions occurred in the spa, where we were almost assured privacy.

Most of our couples spent many nights talking in bed. It was quiet. The other family members were asleep. The phone and door-bell didn't ring very often. The couples didn't get a lot of sleep, but they did get a lot of work done. And we believe the quietness of night helps control the volume a little too.

Not only do you need privacy, but you both also need to feel safe. You each need to speak the absolute truth in love from your hearts. This is not the time to minimize or criticize another's feelings or perceptions. Feelings and perceptions are real, even those we may not believe are warranted. The goal is to help each other get through them. Make it a point to listen carefully and do your best to affirm your spouse. When possible, thank your husband or wife for telling you the truth. Asking to hear the truth and telling the truth are both difficult, so realize that you're both being extremely vulnerable.

In addition, these conversations must be kept between the two of you. It is difficult enough to try to work through this together without worrying about whomever else might be told. If one of you feels a need to share something your spouse has shared with you, we believe you need that spouse's permission first. However, both of you need to have complete freedom when sharing with the counselor you've sought to help you through this process.

Rebuilding a marriage after infidelity is a long process, and talking together can be the beginning—for both of you. It'll also help carry you through the tougher times. The spouse has issues because of the betrayal, lies, and deception. The infidel has issues because he or she is now vulnerable to the spouse. The spouse is now in possession of some very effective weapons that could easily be turned against the infidel. Your commitment to each other means that you choose to use the knowledge for the good of your marriage, not for its destruction.

Responses to Emotional Outbursts

We would love to open this section with "*If* an emotional outburst occurs …," but we know better. "I didn't even know she knew such words!" "I've never heard him talk that way before!" "This is a person I've never met!" We've heard these statements many times in our groups because, sadly, emotional outbursts will occur. They will not be pretty, and they shock most of us. Intellectually, we know that inside an emotional outburst is a very hurt and angry person. But the reality is that very little, if any, work can be accomplished in an atmosphere of emotional volatility.

If you've just let loose on your spouse, this is a good time for you to call a break. And when you've cooled down, go to your spouse and apologize. Apologize for whatever you said or did that did not help the healing process. We don't believe you need to apologize for the feelings—those are real and true—but you do need to say you're sorry for the way you handled them at that particular moment.

For those of you on the receiving end of the emotional outburst, we encourage you not to react to it. That doesn't mean to walk away and ignore the person; we're asking you to ignore the behavior. Gary took to heart Proverbs 15:1: "A gentle answer turns away wrath, but a harsh word stirs up anger." When Mona lost it, he didn't respond in anger or even hurt. He focused on what she was feeling. He would either acknowledge the feeling ("You are in such pain.") or kindly share truth ("We can't make any progress if you just scream at me. Talk to me. Explain to me. Let's work together."). It was difficult to continue an emotional outburst under those circumstances. Somewhere between his "gentle answer" and the Holy Spirit, Mona could sometimes recover her demeanor.

Responding graciously to an emotional outburst is difficult, to say the least. In addition, we often see infidels do well for a while and then begin responding emotionally themselves. Many times the rationale given for this change in behavior is a desire to try to control the emotional response the spouse is continuing to have to the infidelity. It is as though a specific amount of processing time is allotted and anything beyond that is deemed unacceptable. The message the spouse hears is that it is time to "move on" and "quit dredging up the pain all the time."

What we have observed when this occurs is that while one spouse believes he or she is helping, what in fact happens is that the processing is set back instead. The truth is that no one can control the manner or the time in which another person processes anything, much less a traumatic event. But we can each help the other gain perspective and learn to control our emotions in a healthier manner.

We had to often take the road of what has been called "reflective listening." This is where the listener listens, then restates, or "reflects," the message back to the speaker. It can begin with something like "So you're saying …" We thought we communicated well until we used this technique to help with the emotional tsunami we were experiencing. It was when we found ourselves going back and forth several times that we realized maybe we didn't communicate so well. We both had times of sitting with our mouths open at what the other had heard us say. But we'd just keep repeating and explaining until we both understood the same thing.

The other suggestion we have is that you communicate about yourself. We strongly discourage conveying to your mate what you believe they are or are not thinking. When somebody tries to tell you about yourself, it can be a rapid run to your defense table. If you want to convey how you felt when someone behaved a certain way, start with "I" and stay focused on what you saw, felt, or heard.

The goal is for both of you to move through this recovery and end up with a relationship you're able to enjoy together. Talk to one another. Keep it private. Help each other process through at your own speed and in your own way. Focus on maintaining that environment for healing. It's worth it!

Questions for Consideration and Conversation

1. Mona was surprised when she didn't want to talk about the adultery anymore. What do you think helped her get to a point of not needing to talk or ask questions?

2. When Gary questioned whether or not Mona's question was healthy or beneficial to healing, he would ask her if she really wanted to hear the answer. Why do you think that worked? Can you think of other ways to handle the same situation that would benefit the healing process?

3. Why is it common for infidels to resist talking and answering questions about the adultery?

4. Why is it common for a spouse to feel a need to talk about the infidelity and ask the same question over and over again?

5. Resentment is anger with a history. Which do you fear more, resentment or anger? Why?

6. There are differences of opinion on how much detail should be shared with the spouse. Discuss how you as a couple are dealing with this issue and why it is or is not working.

7. Do you believe that your spouse is keeping your conversations private? Is this important to you?

8. We discussed calling a time-out, using reflective listening, and focusing on communicating about yourself. Where are you doing well and where do you need to improve?

9. Read Ephesians 4:15. What are we instructed to do and what is the benefit?

10. Read Proverbs 14:17 and 15:1. How can you apply these in your recovery and why would you want to?

9

Forgiveness

*For if you forgive men when they
sin against you, your heavenly
Father will also forgive you.*

Matthew 6:14

GARY'S STORY
(Shortly after revelation)

It was one of those rare mornings that I actually had a chance to get alone with God and have some quiet time. Mona and I were still fresh in the recovery process. It had been only a few weeks since the night I'd come home and confessed my affair. Mona was spending more mornings sleeping in than not. But hey, after what I'd put her through, it seemed like the least I could do was to let her sleep in when we'd had a rough night. So I had gotten the kids up and off to school.

There I was, alone with God, using daily devotional material that I was way behind on. I had missed these times with God. Then it struck me: The one thing that I had regained was my relationship with the Lord. The sin in my life had done away with any kind of a closeness I'd felt with God. But since I had confessed it and repented, I was again sensing His presence. Today, I actually felt pretty good. I was connecting with my Lord, and it felt wonderful.

I heard the bedroom door open at the end of the hall and saw Mona walk by. She headed into the kitchen in search of her first cup of coffee. This was my wife. She looked like she had been beaten to a pulp and then left for dead. There wasn't even an attempt to muster a "Good morning." Guess I should forget the "good"; we were barely doing "morning" these days.

Last night's conversation came flooding back to my mind. We'd started talking after the kids were in bed. I couldn't even remember now what specifics we had been discussing, but I had hesitated and gotten my thoughts together prior to my answer. She had spent those same moments imagining the worst. It spiraled down from there. She had cried herself to sleep—again. I lay there awake, staring into the darkness of a bedroom that seemed as cold and damp as a tomb. I wondered if this room would ever again be warmed with happiness.

I watched Mona as she successfully navigated her way to the coffeepot, poured her coffee, and returned to the bedroom. I heard the door close behind her.

I was alone again, yet I could still sense the presence of God. I felt forgiven by Him. I really did! I didn't deserve it, but it was a gift I would gratefully receive.

I also somehow knew that Mona was going to forgive me too. I didn't know how I knew, but at that moment I was certain that she would forgive me. I knew if we just stuck it out, she would not only stay with me but also someday forgive me for what I did to her. I welled up with emotion: love and thanksgiving for God and for Mona.

Then the memory of Mona walking into the kitchen flashed through my brain. Mona was a basket case. Last night she once again had her heart ripped out of her chest. And I was the cause. She couldn't have gotten three hours of sleep all night. Yet here I was, welled up with emotion just knowing that God had forgiven me and that she would someday forgive me too. It didn't seem right. I certainly didn't deserve it. How could she forgive me after what I'd done to her?

My prayers turned somber. *God, thank You for Your amazing grace and Your faithfulness to forgive. Lord, thank You for a truly loving wife. With Your help, I know she will forgive me for the foul deeds I've done. But, Lord, oh Lord! How will I ever forgive myself? How do I extend to myself the very gift You offered me?*

This was something I hadn't considered. Me forgiving me? I couldn't! I wouldn't! Since we had started on this path, I had considered what it would be like if Mona had had the affair. I'd quickly pushed those thoughts from my mind because I wasn't sure I would even want to try to rebuild if that were the case. Then I'd felt even guiltier. How could I possibly forgive myself for what I'd done? I had thought I was a better man. So had Mona. I had committed a terrible and destructive sin against God, my wife, everyone. Forgive myself?

The wonderful feelings I had experienced just moments before were gone.

Mona's Story

(More than one year after revelation)

I was going to do it.

I had tried everything else I knew. Maybe this would help. I had to do something. Every Sunday was just like the one before. I determined to do better. I endeavored to be what I claimed to be—a Christian. I wanted to obey God in this adultery recovery process. I wanted to rebuild my marriage. And Gary and I were making progress. It wasn't fun, but it was progress.

It was here at church that I didn't seem to move forward. This was where I saw Gary's partner and her husband every Sunday—or spent the entire morning hoping not to see them. I knew God wanted me to forgive her. I knew I wanted to do what God wanted me to do. I also knew that if we measured injuries, Gary's injury to me had been far worse than her injury to me. But why didn't it feel that way?

I had met with her a few times. It didn't seem to help—and in fact a couple of times, I'd had to call her afterward and apologize for my behavior. I didn't like who I became when she was around. And it wasn't just emotions; I actually had a physical response—uncontrollable shaking, heart palpitations. It took all I had not to run in the opposite direction.

I told myself that unlike my relationship with Gary, his partner and I didn't have unresolved issues. I had thought we were friends, but I was wrong. She had been Gary's "friend." And to top it off, she hadn't seemed to want, much less need, my forgiveness.

Why couldn't I feel that way too? Why couldn't I just not need or want her to ask for forgiveness? I knew the answer: I was being disobedient.

So I had a problem, and I had to try something else to move me forward on this road. That was why I called her husband. I had met with everyone involved in this horror story except him. I dialed, terrified she would answer the phone. She didn't. He agreed to meet me for coffee at a local restaurant. I knew he was curious. So was I. I didn't know what I expected, only that I needed something to help me and that I had exhausted all other possibilities.

We sat at a table. Both of us wary of the other. Once we started talking, we got more comfortable with each other. We ended up sitting there for quite a long time. Questions. Answers. The conversation wandered to repentance and forgiveness. I sat there in shock as I heard him say he didn't believe Gary had truly repented or asked for forgiveness. I tried to look calm on the outside and listen, but inside my head I remembered what it had taken for Gary to call this man soon after revelation and arrange a meeting with him. I remembered praying as Gary walked out the door to one of the most difficult meetings in his life. We had discussed it at length. Her husband had every right to confront Gary. And Gary had an obligation to obey the Scripture passage that says if you have sinned against a fellow brother, you are to go to him. (See Matthew 5:23–24.) Gary had also made a couple of other attempts to facilitate healing—a phone call, a letter. Somehow this man had missed seeing Gary's heart.

And then it hit me. I saw the evidence of Gary's repentance. This man did not. I had read the letter Gary had sent to him. How could he have missed Gary's heart? Was it possible that I was doing the same thing with "her"? Had I missed *her* heart?

I left that meeting with new possibilities ringing in my head. Maybe my lack of progress had more to do with me than it did with her. Maybe *I* was the obstacle in the way.

The Story on Forgiveness

Opinions on forgiveness flow freely. We, like many others, had some preconceived ideas about forgiveness. And we didn't always agree. In fact, many don't agree. So what were we to do in the midst of this storm in which forgiveness was undeniably a major force?

Forgiveness for adultery involves several things. It's not just the spouse forgiving the infidel or the spouse forgiving the partner for damages done to their families. It's also the infidel forgiving the spouse for unmet needs—real or perceived—and the infidel forgiving himself or herself for choosing adultery. It's both of you forgiving one another and yourselves for the weaknesses that contributed to the situation you are now in.

Identifying these areas takes time. Just about the time you think you've at least identified where you need to work, God graciously brings another area to light. The whole issue becomes overwhelming and confusing.

The dictionary states forgiveness is "to cease to demand a penalty for, to cease to blame." [1] In the Bible, the words translated *forgive* mean "to send away, to release or set free." [2] A summary of these definitions is *letting go of the resentment for being wronged.* Charles Stanley states forgiveness involves three elements:

1. Acknowledgment that an injury has occurred.
2. Recognizing that a debt is owed as a result of that wrong done against you.
3. Cancellation of the debt.

He goes on to say forgiving is an act of setting someone free from an obligation to you that is a result of a wrong done against you. [3]

We struggle sometimes because we haven't allowed ourselves to acknowledge the injury. We think we have no right to feel the way we do. Or even in some cases, the one who injured us denies there was an injury, and we vacillate between acknowledging it and denying it. The problem is that if we never acknowledge the injury and never recognize that someone does owe a debt as a result of that injury, we cannot cancel the debt. We cannot send away or release something we have never held.

Sometimes we struggle with forgiveness because of preconceptions we've had over what forgiveness really is. So let's look at what forgiveness is *not* to better bring home the truth of what forgiveness is.

What Forgiveness Is Not

Forgiveness is not containing or restraining our hurt and anger. It is not pretending those feelings are not there. Sometimes we think good Christians don't feel anger or don't incur a debt in response to an injury, as if the Holy Spirit makes everything just bounce off and not penetrate. Not true. Remember Christ in the temple when the people were misusing the temple courts? (See John 2:13–16.)

Forgiveness is not letting someone off the moral hook. We don't ignore or disregard the wrong done. We don't say, "It wasn't that big of a deal. It didn't cause that much damage." And it certainly does not cancel the person's accountability before God. (See Romans 14:12.)

Forgiveness is not an excuse. It is not a suggestion that if we could truly understand the other's viewpoint, we could see he or she had no alternative. We don't say, "I understand why. It was a natural response to how you were treated." Understanding motives and reasons can help us process, but that is not forgiveness.

Forgiveness is not forgetting or some kind of sentimental amnesia. We don't say, "I don't even think about it." We can't forget. The Scripture that states God "remembers" our sins no more (Isaiah 43:25 and Hebrews 8:12) means He doesn't call them to mind, doesn't reflect on them. It's not that He is incapable of remembering.

Forgiveness is not trust. These are two separate issues. I can forgive someone for recklessly smashing my car, but that does not mean I'll hand that person the keys to my new car and put my children in the backseat. That would imply I trust them. Trust requires the cooperation of more than one person. Forgiveness does not.

And finally, *forgiveness is not reconciliation.* Reconciliation means that after a breakdown in a relationship, something has changed and the friendship has been resumed. You can forgive without wanting or accomplishing reconciliation.

What Forgiveness Is

Forgiveness is an issue between you and God. Beth Moore says "forgiveness involves my handing over to God the responsibility for justice."[4]

That's hard. It's against our nature. We struggle with forgiveness because the wrongs done to us by others hurt so much. We want those who hurt us to hurt like us.

It's not so much that we are unable to forgive, but rather we are afraid of what forgiveness might cost us. We do not want to be exploited or appear foolish. And forgiveness is indeed easier if someone wants to be forgiven.

Forgiveness is a big issue. If you are actively involved in this struggle, you know that. And just not thinking about the problem does not make it go away. A pastor friend once told Mona that behind most spiritual problems is a forgiveness issue. We believe that.

So what do we do? How do we as Christians handle this big issue? How do we handle very real and tangible injuries such as adultery?

We asked those questions. Mona especially struggled here. God took her on a journey to see what He had to say about forgiveness so she could correct some of those misconceptions. We'd like to share with you what we have learned from our study of Scripture. Regardless of how you respond to what you learn, you will know the truth about forgiveness.

Matthew 6:9–13 contains teachings by Jesus on how to pray. He said, "This, then, is how you should pray: 'Our Father in heaven, hallowed be your name, your kingdom come, your will be done on earth as it is in heaven. Give us today our daily bread. Forgive us our debts, as we also have forgiven our debtors. And lead us not into temptation, but deliver us from the evil one.'"

We often stop there, but Jesus didn't. In verses 14–15, He explained the relationship between our forgiveness of others and His forgiveness of us: "For if you forgive men when they sin against you, your heavenly Father will also forgive you. But if you do not forgive men their sins, your Father will not forgive your sins."

Remember we said the word *forgive* in Scripture means "to send away, to release or set free"? Jesus taught that to disobey in this respect—to not forgive—is to ensure that what we need to be sent away—our sins—will stay with us. We'll be living with them day after day.

Who was Jesus talking to? If we go back up to Matthew 5:1, we see He was talking to believers: His disciples, His children. Remember, the prayer is directed to "our Father." This is not a passage on salvation but on living as a believer.

Unforgiveness blocks joy and peace. It interferes with your relationship with God. Could the temptation mentioned in 6:13 be to withhold forgiveness? "And lead us not into temptation" follows directly after the line about God forgiving us as we forgive others. Does not forgiving give Satan easier access to us? We believe it does. Satan continually seeks to disrupt our relationship with our heavenly Father. Anytime we disobey God, or sin, it distances us from our Lord. Christ came to reconcile us to God. He also came to reconcile us to one another.

Let's look at Matthew 18:23–35, the parable of the unmerciful servant. Jesus used a story to illustrate a truth.

Verses 23–27: "Therefore, the kingdom of heaven is like a king who wanted to settle accounts with his servants. As he began the settlement, a man who owed him ten thousand talents was brought to him. Since he was not able to pay, the master ordered that he and his wife and his children and all that he had be sold to repay the debt. The servant fell on his knees before him. 'Be patient with me,' he begged, 'and I will pay back everything.' The servant's master took pity on him, canceled the debt and let him go."

"Ten thousand talents" was an enormous debt that the servant genuinely owed.

Verses 28–30: "But when that servant went out, he found one of his fellow servants who owed him a hundred denarii. He grabbed him and began to choke him. 'Pay back what you owe me!' he demanded. His fellow servant fell to his knees and begged him, 'Be patient with me, and I will pay you back.' But he refused. Instead, he went off and had the man thrown into prison until he could pay the debt."

This amount was small in comparison to what the first servant owed. The one who had just been graciously given mercy denied the same to another. Both of these men were guilty. Both owed a debt.

As Christians, we have been forgiven a very large debt. We are unable to comprehend the debt, much less the mercy and its cost.

Verses 31–34: "When the other servants saw what had happened, they were greatly distressed and went and told their master everything that had happened. Then the master called the servant in. 'You wicked servant,' he said, 'I canceled all that debt of yours because you begged me to. Shouldn't you have had mercy on your fellow servant just as I had on you?' In anger his master turned him over to the jailers to be tortured, until he should pay back all he owed."

This servant was jailed and handed over to the jailers to be tortured.

Verse 35 is Jesus' concluding statement: "This is how my heavenly Father will treat each of you unless you forgive your brother from your heart."

Unforgiveness ensures being tortured. Think about the embittered people you know. They are even more miserable than those around them.

How do we make sure this doesn't happen to us? We must forgive. So with this in mind, we offer you two reasons to forgive.

Forgive to obey God.

Forgive to free yourself from oppression.

We realize we're not asking you to do an easy task, but we'd like to give you five realistic, practical things you can begin right now that will lead you toward forgiveness.

Focus on You and Your Relationship with God

Biblical forgiveness is not a human function. You may have to begin by asking God to give you the desire to be obedient. There's no sense in pretending. He knows how you feel. Ask Him to empower you to be the Christian He has called you to be. Admit you don't want to do this. Talk to Him and allow Him the opportunity to talk to you. Changing your heart is His job, and He is capable of doing it.

Spend time in God's Word. Look up everything you can find on forgiveness. Look in your Bible's concordance and read the verses—there are many. Read one or two at a time and talk to Him about what He has said. Ask for understanding. Repeat these truths to yourself until you recognize them as truths.

Recognize and Acknowledge the Hurt and the Pain

An injury has occurred; denying it only gives that pain more power and creates a barrier to forgiveness. If you cannot share your hurt because sharing will evoke too much pain, then you know it is an infected wound, painful even to the touch. As we both worked through the hurt and pain, it began to ease. Now it is a sad memory. We'll never be okay about what happened, but we can heal. Acknowledging the hurt and pain is a first step in that direction.

We're not talking about sharing to cause pain to the person who inflicted your pain. You may need to share your pain with God alone or with a Christian counselor. This is not negating some of the other principles we've talked about. The point here is to identify and recognize it. Some people in pain have written down everything in vivid, horrid detail and then burned the document. Mona spent some time writing down just how she felt about what God had allowed. She wrote in explicit detail what she was thinking about everything and everyone involved—then added what she thought should happen now. Not very pretty words at all. But each time she finished, exhausted by the emotional effort, she burned those words and asked God to give her His perspective. It also helped her identify areas requiring forgiveness that were not so obvious. The point is to clean out the wound—as if it were a pocket of infection. Then treat it with the balm of God's healing touch so that it can heal.

Let Go of the Blame

Letting go of the blame is so difficult. We want to know why this terrible thing has happened to us. Blame seeks to find the culprit, to assign the role of villain. If we can just do that, then maybe we can keep it from ever happening again.

The reality is that we will never find a good enough reason for some of the wrongs done to us because there is not any one reason. Even as important as it was for us to work through the circumstances and issues that brought us here, neither of us found "the answer" or "the reason" Gary chose to risk everything for an affair. He just did. Mona had to accept that as fact so she could move forward.

See the Other Person as a Person of Value

Every human being is precious in God's eyes. Every human being was created in God's image. Jesus died for us all, not just those we would consider "worth it."

That means that when we look at the person who caused our pain, we do not look at only a liar, cheater, or destroyer. When Mona had occasion to see Gary's partner, she had to practice reminding herself that she was looking at a woman who was loved by God, not just at the woman who had an affair with her husband. It meant that when she looked at this woman, her entire estimation of her was not based only on a sin. We do not determine another person's value; God does.

Work Toward Forgiveness

Forgiveness is a goal to pursue, not a prize to grasp. We may repeatedly lose and gain ground. Forgiveness is hard work. We want it to be instantaneous—like microwave oatmeal. That would be nice, but it is not reality. About the time we think we've gotten it down, we'll find ourselves in the midst of it again. Satan would love to use that against us, telling us we aren't forgiving, that we are failures as Christians. Because we're believers, he can't have us back, but he can make us miserable. Don't let the work of forgiveness detour you. You are making progress. We don't believe that is failure. We believe that is obedience. And it is worth it!

Forgiveness is a process. Give yourself some grace as you process through the emotions.

Forgiveness is a direction you are taking. Keep walking toward it.

Forgiveness is a gift you can give and a gift you can receive.

Forgiveness is a choice—no one can make you do this. The question is "will you walk the path according to God or according to you?"

You need God now more than at any other time in your life. Don't block your relationship with Him. Don't travel this road alone. When we are obedient to God, He rewards us. Choosing this path out of obedience is a major step toward rekindling the love and trust that have been damaged. Feelings often follow our actions and come behind our obedience. Trust God. He is trustworthy.

Questions for Consideration and Conversation

1. Gary struggled with forgiving himself. What are some of the things that make forgiving ourselves difficult?

2. Mona realized that perhaps she was the one blocking her ability to forgive Gary's partner. Do you believe a request for forgiveness is required to obey God's command to forgive?

3. What has been your definition of forgiveness?

4. Discuss what forgiveness is not. Which of these misconceptions have been part of your thinking?

5. The two passages we looked at from Scripture gave us God's perspective on forgiveness. Did you gain any new insights?

6. We suggested you forgive in obedience to God and to free yourself from oppression. Do you agree? Why or why not?

7. Are you able to focus on your relationship with God? What could your spouse do to help?

8. Have you been able to acknowledge the hurt and pain while letting go of the blame? What is your biggest struggle?

9. Can you see the person you need to forgive as a person of value in God's eyes?

10. Forgiveness is work. Why do you think that is true or not true?

10

Rebuilding Trust

Surely God is my salvation; I
will trust and not be afraid.
The LORD, the LORD, is my
strength and my song.
Isaiah 12:2

MONA'S STORY

(About six months after revelation)

"Mom, when is dinner going to be ready? I'm hungry."

I looked down at my seven-year-old son. He was always the one who needed to eat.

I looked at the clock—again. Almost six. Where was Gary? He said he'd be home at five thirty.

Gary and I were several months into our adultery recovery and it seemed more like years to both of us. I'd finally had a little bit of energy to spare, so I'd made a nice dinner. These occasions were few and far between lately. If I thought about how much junk food and television the kids had … well, I couldn't go there. There was enough guilt and pain already. And like our counselor said, if we don't get Mom and Dad healthy, there's not a lot to offer the kids.

I gave my unhappy son a carrot stick and sent him back to play with his brothers, telling him Dad would be home soon and we'd eat then.

Where could Gary be? I reached for the phone to call the office and remembered I'd already done that—twice. The first time, they said Gary had already left. The second, no answer.

What if he's been in an accident? I reached to get a glass of water for my dry throat and noticed my hand shaking so much the water sloshed in the glass. I could hear the blood pounding in my ears and wondered what my blood pressure might be. *You have got to get a handle on yourself. You're really overreacting. He's a little late. Maybe traffic is heavy.*

But it takes only ten minutes to get home and it had been fifteen minutes since the second call, not to mention the first that was twenty-five minutes ago.

I found myself staring out the kitchen window, searching for car lights. Each time I saw headlights, I would tense, hoping to see them turn into our driveway. Then that tension bled into disappointment when the car lights kept on going past our home.

Gary had always been considerate to check in with me if he was going to be delayed. In fact that had been one of the surprises about the adultery. I always knew—thought I knew—where he was. But since revelation, he'd tried to be even more accountable. He checked in with me often. Anything that might keep him away was explained in detail. I don't think I'd really even noticed until tonight—when he hadn't.

Why hasn't he called to let me know he'll be late? And if he's working late, why isn't he answering the phone?

I shouldn't have been surprised by the path my thoughts scurried down. Nothing surprised me anymore. Except me—*I* surprised me all the time. I'd never been a jealous person. Never worried about what Gary was or wasn't doing. I'd trusted him with all I had. I'd trusted him with me.

What if they're together? They could be kissing right now. He could be holding her and touching her while you stand here like little Suzy Housewife, "Oh, honey, dinner's ready." Stupid idiot. Dumb. What made you think he would tell you the truth now?

Stop it! Stop it! My hands clenched into fists so tight I could feel my nails cutting into my palms in an attempt to block the thoughts from continuing. It didn't work.

Like you can tell if he's lying? He's probably been lying this whole time. Amazing he could even keep up with both of you at once. Well, maybe not. He's been doing it for three years.

I grabbed the dishcloth and started wiping the counters as if my life depended on it. Maybe not my life. Maybe just my sanity.

The sound of a car driving by drew my attention back to the window and I watched as it continued down the street.

So do you think he's going to come in here and confess? Oh, no. He'll come in with some excuse, some story. And you won't know if it's true. You'll never know until he sits down on the bed again....

I held my hands over my ears, willing my thoughts to stop, knowing I was teetering on a sinkhole to destruction. I didn't know what would be destroyed first, my marriage or me.

I realized I'd never really known where Gary was. I just thought I knew. The truth was I never really knew for sure where anyone was. Including my kids. I did everything I could to keep them safe— checking in with other parents, dropping off, picking up. But the reality was from the time I watched my kids walk away until the time I saw them return, I only thought I knew where they were. How many parents are surprised to find out their kids went somewhere else when they were supposed to be in another place? We don't know for sure unless we're with them.

Calm down. Deep breaths. Relax. I felt my heart slow down and become more regular. I folded the dishcloth over the sink and sat at the kitchen table.

Okay, what was I going to do with this? As I saw it, I had three choices:

1. I could go crazy every time he's not by my side.
2. I could leave, divorce, and never have to worry about whether he's lied to me again.
3. I could choose to give him another chance.

Because eventually it would always come down to this. Trusting him again was not just about him being trustworthy; it was also about me recognizing there'd be times my trust would be required. Like tonight, when he's twenty-five—make that twenty-eight— minutes late.

When he walks in the door, I'll ask why he's late and he'll offer an explanation. He can terminate the rebuilding of trust by refusing to explain, or I can terminate the rebuilding of trust by refusing to listen.

Oh, Lord, help us, help me, do this. I want my marriage to heal. I think Gary does too. Help me to do my part in this.

I suddenly experienced a calm that flowed through my body. My heart no longer pounded. The battle in my mind ceased. There is a peace God sometimes gives that defies explanation, and that is what I felt when I prayed that night.

About five minutes later Gary's car turned in the driveway.

GARY'S STORY

(About six months after revelation and the same night as Mona's story)

It was a great day at work. One of those days when everything I touched just seemed to turn to gold. Every task complete, every client happy.

I stuck my head in the control room on my way out to say good night to the engineer, but he was busy setting up with a few of the band members who had a recording session booked for the night. That brought a smile and some great memories of when I was the studio engineer.

As I walked out the door, the warm evening air was a bit of a surprise. I could smell the orchard just behind the studio. It smelled good.

I felt good. Something of a rarity these days. It had been almost six months since revelation, and Mona and I were starting to settle down a bit. We were working hard. I was trying to do everything right—finally. And I was beginning to see a glimmer of hope in Mona's eyes.

As I slipped into the driver's seat, I rolled down the window to enjoy the breeze on the short drive home. I enjoyed feeling good for a change. It had been the roughest few months of my life.

Coming down the road toward home, I caught the Radio Shack store out of the corner of my eye. I needed solder. I had been working on a ham radio project the last couple of weeks. A rediscovered hobby that I had been enjoying since my secret double life had come to an end. Getting back into a hobby had provided me with some time to relax and just not think.

My friend Brian was working the counter when I dropped the solder down for him to ring up. "Need anything else, Gary?"

"Nope, that's it."

Brian was about ten years younger than me and a real radio buff. He was fully aware of my career in radio broadcasting and loved to just talk shop whenever I came into the store. "Have you heard the new radio station in town, Gary?"

That's all it took for me. I started in on the full description of their new format and how creative it sounded. Quite frankly it felt good to talk to somebody who didn't know about my personal life.

After a few minutes of doing some real quality "tech talk," a couple of people came into the store needing help so I said my good-byes and headed for the car.

When I pulled into the driveway, I noticed Mona looking out the kitchen window. As I walked in and made my way into the kitchen I could tell she had been crying. "What's wrong?" I asked.

"Nothing!" she snapped.

"Come on, I can tell something is bothering you."

"If you don't know …"

"If I don't know what? What happened?"

My mind raced, taking a mental inventory of the day. When I left this morning, she was fine. She seemed even a little bit happy. I called at least three times throughout the day and hadn't picked up on anything being wrong.

"I really don't know what you are talking about."

She looked up at me with a hard, cold stare. "Where have you been?"

"I've been at work. I haven't been anywhere else. I swear to you."

"I have been trying to call you for over twenty minutes. They said you left a half hour ago." She was obviously working to control herself. Her words were deliberately paced and her tone even. "And it doesn't take a half hour to drive the three miles to home. Where have you been?"

The light came on in my head. Radio Shack. Brian. Just how long had I been there? I rushed to explain. "I stopped by Radio Shack and got some solder for my ham radio kit. Brian was working tonight and we got into a conversation about the new radio station."

She slowly got up from the table and walked back into our bedroom, closing the door behind her, her face a confusing twist of emotions. I could see the battle waging within her trying to find truth.

Trust. Something I'd never appreciated having until I lost it completely. Back before revelation, a half hour spent with a friend "shooting the breeze" would not have been a big deal. But in the light of our current situation, it was a huge issue.

Mona was hypersensitive to every minute I was outside her radar. I supposed I could get defensive and say that I couldn't live like this for the rest of my life, but quite frankly I didn't blame her at all. It wasn't like I'd had massive amounts of time unaccounted for while I was involved in an affair.

But how was she ever going to trust me again? In fact if I thought about it too much I had to wonder if I'd be able to trust myself ever again.

But I'd changed. I'd truly repented. And I was doing everything I could think of to heal this marriage.

I knew she would also have a hard time trusting herself. She'd told me her instincts, her "woman's intuition," had failed her miserably.

I knew neither one of us could live like this for the rest of our lives.

The good day I'd had began to fade with the closing of the bedroom door.

THE STORY ON REBUILDING TRUST

Rebuilding trust is an essential part of healing after infidelity because a healthy marriage requires trust. We can facilitate the rebuilding of trust, which is not easy. Or we can tear down the fragile beginnings of that process, which is far too easy.

We chose to rebuild the trust.

Mona had to redefine what trust looked like in a healthy marriage. After much soul-searching she came to realize she had trusted Gary partially because she believed she'd be able to "know" when or if he was no longer trustworthy. That meant she felt safe trusting him more because of herself rather than whether or not he was trustworthy. She didn't understand that trusting him really meant putting herself at risk. Her sense of safety rested within a power she actually did not have.

Think of it this way. In a car equipped for training drivers, there is a brake pedal for the driver and a brake pedal for the trainer on the passenger side of the car. The primary pedal is the one used by the driver in training. But the trainer knows that if the driver errs, he also has the ability to apply the brake on his side of the car and prevent damage or injury. Mona thought she had that same "safety brake" available to her.

This also holds true for those who think that they can rebuild trust in a marriage by controlling their spouse—constantly sitting in that trainer's seat ready to apply the brakes if their husband or wife makes a wrong turn. No one can sit in the trainer's seat forever. Every driver eventually will drive alone.

Let's start with a biblical understanding of trust. The Hebrew and Greek words translated *trust* mean to believe, to uphold, to support. The idea is firmness or solidity; to be persuaded to have confidence in. We feel safe when we can rely on what we trust.

So when we trust, we are saying that we have been firmly persuaded to believe. We choose a specific chair to stand on because we trust it will hold our weight. When we trust our spouse, we believe this person will do what they say they'll do and not do what they say they won't do. The bottom line is we feel safe. Once adultery has been revealed, that is no longer the case.

For several years, Gary had lied to Mona, and not only that, but he had also gotten quite good at it. After the revelation of his adultery, Mona could no longer trust that he would be honest. What he had done caused great harm. The trust Mona had was gone in a few short minutes. The question neither of us had the answer to was "could it ever be regained?"

Gary understood this very well. He told Mona, "I know what I'm asking. Every time you've fallen backward I've caught you. But this time I let you fall on purpose. It wasn't that I missed catching you; it was that I walked away to somewhere else. You hit hard; you were injured. I didn't even notice. And now I come to you and say, 'I'm sorry. It's okay now, honey, just fall back and I'll catch you.'"

Rebuilding the trust meant Mona would have to find a way back to believing with confidence that Gary was a safe person to trust. It also meant she would put herself in a position where Gary could, again, let her fall and be hurt. She wasn't sure she could ever do that. But it was also the only way she would ever be caught by him again.

It's interesting that in Scripture, most of the verses dealing with trust are talking about our trust in the Lord, not in our fellow man. In fact there are several warnings about trusting in anything or anyone else.

The truth is that our God is the only one who is completely trustworthy. He is the only one who will always keep His promises.

But it was also true that Mona had failed Gary too. Just in a different way. Remember, Gary had trusted that Mona would love him as she had promised. At the time of the affair, from Gary's perspective, she had not kept her promise either. Rebuilding the trust meant that Gary would have to believe that Mona would be a safe person to trust again.

Our journeys would be different, but we would both be taking one.

Gary has often heard infidels express that if only their spouse would forgive them, they could move past the adultery. But what they are really saying is "If they would trust me." Trust and forgiveness are two different things. We talked about that in the chapter on forgiveness.

The foundation we rebuild on will be the foundation intended for marriage—God Himself. That foundation is sound because God is trustworthy. We rebuild the trust as if we were rebuilding a house—brick by brick. The house fell, but God's foundation is still safe. The things you do as a couple will, in essence, be handing each other bricks, one at a time, to create a structurally sound house on a firm foundation. One brick at a time until you both learn to function as the team God intended and can begin to sense the safety coming back into your relationship.

The most essential piece in this rebuilding is transparent honesty. We've said it before and we'll keep on saying it. Honesty enables each of you to see the other's heart and paves the way when you hit bumps in the road. Honesty will keep you on the path.

The onus falls on the infidel here. This person sets the stage and the atmosphere. If he or she is willing to share openly about activities, phone calls, travel plans, anything where the spouse is not a participant, he or she has created an opportunity to begin rebuilding trust.

The question that usually comes here is "I'm to be treated like a two-year-old for the rest of my life?" The answer is no—that is what you're trying to prevent. But trust must be rebuilt first.

Trust is earned. Honesty plays a big role in obtaining it.

It's been said that part of a second chance is taking responsibility for the mess you made in the first place. Honestly taking ownership for what you've done to break that trust and what you'll do to rebuild it can encourage a spouse to stay on the path of rebuilding trust with you.

Dr. Doug Rosenau says the "ultimate cause of infidelity is a series of poor choices."[1] If your spouse can be witness to the exploration of those poor choices, what Gary calls the transparent soul-searching of how and why the infidelity happened, it offers both of you an understanding of some reasons you are here. It also helps the spouse begin to see that you really want to change and brings hope you'll never go there again.

We must repeat that there is no reason good enough for the choice of adultery. But figuring out some of those baby steps that led to the affair and why you chose to take them helps you choose a different path the next time similar choices are in front of you. If your spouse has been a part of your thinking this through, they are better able to trust your choices next time.

When Gary realized, in retrospect, how vulnerable he was at the time his affair started, the foolishness of the choices he made before anything romantic happened became clear. As he was able to share those insights with Mona, she was able to begin to relax when wondering if it would happen again. As we talked about what choices could have been made instead and what choices he planned to make in the future, the way out of temptation that God had promised became visible to us both.

That same transparent honesty needs to be a part of the spouse's contribution to rebuilding trust. Mona needed to convey to Gary what this betrayal felt like to her so he could comprehend the consequences of his choices and could understand with empathy the pain his betrayal had caused.

Gary didn't want to focus on what had happened, and he hated to see Mona in pain. This is very common for the infidel, but we encourage you to think of it this way. If every time your spouse wants to talk about it, you shut them down by changing the subject, avoiding the questions, or tap-dancing around the issues, your spouse will hear that you don't care and don't want to change. You just want to move on. And if you're not willing to change, how will they ever trust you again? That is why it is so important to process through this together as a couple.

The other aspect of transparent honesty Mona had to accept was the fact that in the end, she would have to entrust Gary to God and place herself in a position of vulnerability. That was part of what happened the night Gary came home late. Just as much as Gary needed to be accountable to rebuild the trust, she needed to be willing to accept the efforts he was making. Rebuilding trust was a process for her, too. As Gary made deposits in trustworthiness, she would have to credit them to his account.

The final piece we'll suggest is almost too simple. Adopt an attitude that every little thing counts. It all adds up to rebuilding trust.

Gary talks a lot to infidels about getting behind the eyes of their spouse, seeking to understand the things that make a person feel safe and comprehending that some things, even things that are unintentional, can feel like a threat. Like Gary coming home late.

Trust can be lost in an instant—not rebuilt that way. To consistently build trust, you need lots of opportunities to come through. So create them for yourself. Do what you say you're going to do. If something changes, call and explain why. If you say you'll pick up milk on the way home, pick up milk on the way home. Coming home without the milk becomes something far more than forgetting to stop at the store. It easily becomes another example of why you can't be trusted.

Every lie, no matter how trivial, counts.

Every omission of fact counts.

The process is slow and requires both of you. The spouse needs to acknowledge and give credit for the things the infidel does to rebuild that trust. If we refuse to credit a kept promise because "that's what you should have done in the first place," the motivation to continue trying wanes. We all need to know that what we're doing counts.

One of the most common areas we see this is when there is an unplanned contact between the infidel and their partner. Maybe the partner contacted them or a work situation put them together. The one who has been unfaithful is trying to be honest and rebuild trust, so they come home and say the words they know will upset their spouse.

For those of us who have been in that spouse's position, we know there's a little voice in our heads that admonishes us for believing. That tells us we're fools. And we know that our spouse is capable of lying to us. But if it's the truth and we tear into the one trying to rebuild, then we are the ones destroying the trust. And the one who was unfaithful will begin to doubt the value of being honest in everything. If the infidel gets beat up every time they're honest, they will eventually quit being honest. Remember the importance of creating that environment for healing.

Mona prayed that truth would be revealed. And it was. As time went on, her anxiety decreased and she became capable once more of believing Gary.

Trust does not require blinders. We trust someone because we now choose to believe they will make the right choice. And we believe that because there has been evidence of those right choices.

Rebuilding trust is a risk for both of you. Each will make small steps forward as you see progress being made. Each fears what the future will look like.

The one thing we are confident of is if either one of you is unwilling to do the work required to rebuild trust, then the hole vacated by the trust will only grow bigger.

But if you'll work together, take the risk, and create the environment for healing, then you, too, can rebuild the trust that was lost. And the wound of adultery, although huge, will not be fatal.

C. S. Lewis explains beautifully why we work to rebuild trust: "To love at all is to be vulnerable. Love anything, and your heart will certainly be wrung and possibly broken. If you want to make sure of keeping it intact, you must give your heart to no one, not even to an animal. Wrap it carefully round with hobbies and little luxuries; avoid all entanglements; lock it up safe in the casket or coffin of your selfishness. But in that casket—safe, dark, motionless, airless—it will change. It will not be broken; it will become unbreakable, impenetrable, irredeemable.... The only place outside Heaven where you can be perfectly safe from all the dangers ... of love is Hell."[2]

Questions for Consideration and Conversation

1. Mona struggled when Gary was late arriving home. What did she fear and why? Was it reasonable after several months of recovery?

2. Gary didn't understand his being late would cause Mona concern. What could he have done differently to quell her worries?

3. What has been your understanding of trust in a marriage?

4. Feeling safe is a big part of rebuilding trust. Discuss things that would make you feel safe in this recovery process.

5. Do you agree that trusting someone means you are vulnerable? Why or why not?

6. Talk about "transparent honesty" from the perspective of your role. "As the spouse that means I would …" or "As the infidel that means I would …"

7. Talk about how you will respond to the transparent honesty from your mate. Can you think of any methods of preparation that would help you do this?

8. Read Psalm 62:5–8. What hope does God offer you?

9. Every little thing counts. Share with your spouse a "little thing" they have done that has helped you.

10. Read the quote by C. S. Lewis together. Share your thoughts.

11
Hedges

Therefore I will block her
path with thornbushes; I
will wall her in so that she
cannot find her way.
Hosea 2:6

MONA'S STORY

(More than three years after revelation)

It had been a really nice evening. We were with two other couples, and we always did a lot of laughing when the six of us got together. Dinner had been delicious, and as usual I'd eaten way too much. I settled back into the large, soft sofa and just listened to the others banter.

I wasn't sure how the conversation had gotten there, but I realized Gary was saying something about not lunching alone with a female. One friend seemed a bit surprised by this and asked Gary what he did when business needed to be accomplished and lunch was suggested. Gary replied that he met the woman in the office or went to lunch in a group, just never him and another woman alone.

Then our friend asked Gary why he did this. Now it was my turn to be surprised. This friend knew about Gary's affair. He'd watched us go through a good part of our recovery process.

Gary replied, "I don't want to be alone with another woman. I don't want to start a friendship with another woman and find myself sharing things and developing a relationship that could turn intimate. That was one of the things that started me down the path of adultery, and I never want to go there again."

"You think because you have lunch with a woman you're going to have an affair?"

"Of course not," Gary replied. "It's just a safety net I use so that I'll never be in a position again to start down that path."

I could tell our friend thought Gary was being paranoid. I thought about every infidel we'd had in our groups. Almost all the affairs had developed out of a business or ministry relationship. People thought they were so above this thing called adultery. They thought they were stronger than that. Gary had thought the same thing.

I had always had that safety net. I always avoided one-on-one social situations with other men. In a hospital setting it was easy to do.

Then our friend looked at me.

"Would you go to lunch with me?"

"No," I said with a smile.

I could see his brain working to find some way to catch me in what he considered my foolishness.

"What if I asked you to go to the mall and help me pick out a gift for my wife—would you meet with me then?"

"Gary and I would be happy to help you pick out a gift for your wife."

"You wouldn't go to the mall with me and help me pick out something for my wife?"

"Not alone. I'd go with another female friend or with Gary, and we'd all help you pick out that gift."

"I can't believe you wouldn't even go to the mall with me. It's a public place!"

How could I make him understand what we were saying? I knew we were frustrating him something awful.

"Look, you're my friend. We have good times together as couples. You and I have some great conversations. I don't want to mess that up. It's not that I think we couldn't go to the mall without having an affair—of course we could. It's not the one-time thing. It's creating a situation where you and I start to have a special bond that doesn't include our spouses. I personally don't think men and women can have intimate friendships without taking a risk I'm unwilling to take. I know some people do, and nothing ever develops beyond that friendship. Others, though, thought the same thing and ended up with a lot more than a friendship. In my opinion, that risk is too high and the cost is too great. And quite frankly, I don't think anyone is exempt. I believe any person, given the right time, the right set of circumstances, and the right person can fall. I believed that before Gary's affair. I believe it even more now."

I could tell he wasn't convinced. The friends in that room all thought Gary and I were being overly sensitive. Well, so be it. We had seen too much. The conversation moved on without any of us changing our minds on this particular subject. Our friend still disagreed. We had shared our opinions, but what others did or did not do was between them, their spouses, and God. Being considered silly or oversensitive was a price we were willing to pay.

Gary's Story
(More than one year after revelation)

I was nervous. The church chairman pulled me aside on Sunday morning and requested a meeting with him and our senior pastor. Was Thursday afternoon at four okay?

"Yeah, sure," I said. I wondered what this was all about. It had been a little over a year since the adultery scandal. Mona and I were getting through each day, one moment at a time. Our counselor had just dropped us down to once a month. *Thank You, God, for small victories.* At least someone thought we were making progress.

After I told Mona about the meeting, we speculated about the possible reasons. They were most certainly *not* going to ask me to serve on any kind of board or ministry. Mona thought maybe they were just going to check on how I was doing.

By Thursday afternoon I was dying of curiosity. What did these two church leaders want with me? I slipped into the room and saw the two of them already seated at a table. I sat down, and the church chairman began the meeting.

"Gary, Pastor and I asked to see you today because we have something important we need to talk about. It's been a year since your confession before God and the pastor. We have discussed your situation with the deacon board, and we unanimously agree that you have shown growth, maturity, and true repentance from your sin. We would like to officially restore you to ministry here at the church."

Relief flooded through me. A positive. Something to smile about. Progress.

I thanked them, we conversed a bit more, and then with smiles and handshakes, we rose to our feet and went our separate ways.

As I drove out of the parking lot, I felt encouraged. That good news had been delivered to me with the utmost respect and satisfaction on their part. It felt good to have somebody trust me again.

But I couldn't help wondering how they knew I was actually better? How could they know? I hadn't even been meeting regularly with the accountability partner they had put me with. I wasn't in a small group. I had no contact with any leader outside the typical Sunday morning smile and handshake. Could they know how I was truly doing with God? They couldn't. But they thought they did. By all outward appearances, I was doing great! I was attending church. Mona and I were still together. But I was still the same Christian guy who had an affair with another woman in the church for three years! And they didn't have a clue then, either.

Don't get me wrong. I wasn't criticizing them. They were just people doing the best they could with the system they had in place. Their hearts and intentions were sincere. And I would learn later that the pastor had checked with our counselor. But driving away that day, I realized the system in place wasn't enough. It wasn't good enough to protect me from myself. It wasn't good enough to ensure faithfulness. The reality was I was right back where I'd started in the church. Nothing had really changed.

I realized that if there was going to be change, I would have to do it. I couldn't rely on my church or its leadership to do it for me. And it wasn't going to happen simply because I wanted it to.

They were right about one thing. My relationship with God was good. That was first and foremost. And I was diligently working on restoring my relationship with Mona. But I knew I needed to do something intentional for myself. I needed to think about how I had gotten here in the first place and what exactly I was going to do to keep myself from ever coming here again.

These were not new thoughts. But what had happened that day scared me. I knew I could be driving out of this same parking lot, picking up the phone to call a mistress. I had expected to feel safer when those around me considered me "safe" again. I'd been wrong.

What little accountability had been in place for the last year was fading. My counselor was phasing us out. My church had ceased its discipline. Even Mona was beginning to relax—a little. But four years ago, I had slipped into sin subtly and slowly and no one had known. It was surprising how easily it happened. How easily I could live a double life. At the time, I thought I was close to God, but I had fallen into Satan's snare just as easily as some dumb animal gets trapped by following its instincts.

I didn't want to be taken by surprise again. And I knew that I would again encounter times when I was vulnerable to temptation.

I thought about the men I'd known throughout my life, men who had cheated, men who had not cheated. There wasn't a huge difference between them. The men I'd known who had been unfaithful to their wives hadn't awakened one morning saying, "I think I'll ruin my marriage."

No, I needed to do some serious thinking. I needed to provide myself with some protection.

THE STORY ON HEDGES

Jerry Jenkins authored a book titled *Hedges: Loving Your Marriage Enough to Protect It.* In it, he talked about "hedges": actions and attitudes we cultivate to protect ourselves and our marriage. Hedges that keep love in and infidelity out.[1]

Human beings are relational. That is how God made us. But marriage is one unique relationship with one special person. Any intrusion into that "relational space" we give to one another in marriage creates an avenue for an illicit relationship. Often we believe that concept relates only to the sexual relationship, but sex is just one part of marriage.

Marriage is the most private, personal, deep, and thorough relationship a person can ever have with another person on this earth. It requires a level of physical, emotional, and spiritual intimacy that asks much from us personally and gives more in return to us individually. A good marriage in the end is worth the vulnerability and risk we open ourselves up to. This overall intimacy in marriage is what we need to protect. Setting aside a spouse and allowing another person to share spiritual or emotional intimacy can destroy a marriage as effectively as becoming sexually intimate with another person. It's just easier to pretend there's not a problem if it is not sexual—yet.

The fact is that very few of us start out to disrupt marital intimacy. Sometimes we simply fail to establish it. Sometimes we fail to maintain it. More often we fail to protect it. "It just happened" is a common explanation for adultery. And it also exposes how little we understand the steps that got us there.

When we have unresolved issues in the marriage, we make it easier to "just happen," and when we don't have appropriate hedges in place, we invite it to happen. This is especially true in our current American culture. We don't have the traditional societal barriers to male-female friendships and interactions. No matter what our thoughts are on this subject, we have to agree that although freedoms we have in a more liberal society have broadened our personal opportunities and enabled us to enjoy a great many more diverse experiences, they have also increased our need for self-imposed hedges.

We'd like to share with you two essential principles that we believe are invaluable to protecting your marriage.

Admit You Are Vulnerable

You are not stronger than anyone else. You are a human being, and people are attracted to each other—we're supposed to be. That is how God created us. It's not a switch you can turn off after the wedding ceremony.

Mona worked in an office about two years into our marriage. Suddenly she found herself looking forward to one particular man's daily check-in. She would be waiting for him when he came. One day, when she found herself in the bathroom primping, she realized what was going on. She had a crush! She was acting like a sixteen-year-old schoolgirl. Fortunately, the gentleman never responded to her unspoken cues, and she got over her crush. But she had to do some serious thinking about just what was going on emotionally and what she would do in the future if she found herself attracted to another man. It could have been a very different scenario if that man had responded differently and Mona hadn't realized what she was in fact doing.

Don't deny an attraction. Admit it to yourself and then run! In fact, we are told in 1 Corinthians 6:18 to "flee from sexual immorality." We don't run from something we do not believe can hurt us. Attractions happen, and they can hurt us if we don't run.

Most counselors agree on a definite turning point in an illicit relationship. It's when the two people involved admit to each other their attraction and vow to fight it. That very act proves to be almost inflaming. *Therefore, we do not advise admitting the attraction to the one you are attracted to. Rather, admit it to yourself—and then run!*

Some advise running to your husband or wife and becoming accountable to them for handling that attraction. Shirley Glass, a noted specialist in adultery, says, "When we share our hidden feelings about another person with our spouse, the intensity and fascination of that secret are greatly diminished. We let reality into fantasy."[2]

Establish Your Hedges Before You Need Them

You have to admit your vulnerability before you can recognize the need for protective measures. Safety glasses were created because someone got hurt. Don't let that someone be you or your spouse.

There are three definite areas that need "hedging" as we seek to protect our marriages.

The Eyes

With our eyes we illuminate the objects of our desires. Keep your eyes where they belong. Appreciating beauty is a natural response to visual stimuli, whether it's a sunset or a gorgeous human being. The difference lies in how long we allow ourselves to focus and what we focus on. Jesus said in Matthew 5:28, "Anyone who looks at a woman lustfully has already committed adultery with her in his heart." The Greek word translated *looks* means to keep on looking and stresses continuous or repeated action. Appreciating an attribute of another person is fine, but make it brief and then move on.

The Actions

James 1:14–15 tells us, "But each one is tempted when, by his own evil desire, he is dragged away and enticed. Then, after desire has conceived, it gives birth to sin; and sin, when it is full-grown, gives birth to death." Desire is "conceived" when we help it happen, when we take things and put them together. When we add our hands or our voice to a desire, we move down that path of temptation. Some of us are touchers by nature. Some of us are complimenters. We need to be aware of how and why we're touching and under what circumstances we're complimenting, as well as what message we're sending.

Are you trying to make yourself attractive to another? If so, you're flirting, and it isn't harmless. Do you look forward to interactions with a particular person of the opposite sex? Be wary. Are you sensing someone else is a little too friendly? Trust your instincts and be cautious.

To avoid being misunderstood and to maintain appropriate emotional and physical distance, some suggest complimenting the tangible, such as hair or clothing, and not the person. Some suggest limiting hugs to a special few and only in the presence of others. There are many ways to express warmth and kindness or respect and admiration without crossing boundaries. Identify as a couple the ways that are comfortable for both of you and stick to them.

The Mind

Sin is born in the mind. When we daydream about a person of the opposite sex who is not our spouse, that is an invitation to sin. When we "innocently" facilitate arrangements to be with someone else, we're already in trouble. Rationalizing your thoughts about another person is deluding yourself. If you find yourself fantasizing or manipulating events, it is time to do a very fast U-turn.

That same mind that leads us down the road of sin can lead us back to God and our spouse. Flirt with your spouse. Daydream about your spouse. Go ahead and look intently on your spouse's attributes. Remember your wedding vows. Is there something you can do today or this week to remind your spouse of the intimate relationship you're called to have together? Think about what attracted you to your spouse in the first place. Focus on what is beautiful in him or her.

If you find these exercises difficult, maybe it's time to sit your spouse down and have a much-needed conversation. Don't let your marriage slide away because of neglect. Spend time with the person you committed to love in a marriage. Some of us have gotten the idea that if love takes work, then it must not be real, and it's certainly not romantic. That is a lie. All relationships require energy and effort. Romance comes when you provide the environment for it.

Are hedges really necessary? Isn't setting them up a little like running scared? We would answer yes to both questions. With more than 50 percent of marriages—Christian and non-Christian—ending in divorce and a society running rampant with sexual immorality, scared is a pretty good thing to be. If you let your guard down, if you don't remind yourself that you made a vow before God to your mate, if you don't set up hedges for your eyes, hands, and voice, and if you let your mind and emotions go their own way, you run a high risk of becoming a statistic.

On the other hand, you can learn from your mistakes. You can incorporate some protective measures into your life. Then maybe you and your spouse can become members of a much smaller demographic: those marriages that not only survived infidelity but also fully healed and remain a relationship both of you will cherish forever.

Questions for Consideration and Conversation

1. Gary realized his accountability needed to ultimately be put in place by him. Describe to your spouse the things you have in place, or will put in place, to provide hedges for you.

2. Mona and Gary's friends thought they were being paranoid. Why wouldn't Mona go to the mall with her friend to help him pick out a gift for his wife?

3. Do you believe a person in a "happy marriage" can be attracted to someone else? Why or why not?

4. Mona and Gary said sometimes couples fail to establish, maintain, or protect the intimate relationship they are to have with one another. Discuss this in relation to your marriage.

5. Discuss some of the things you see in our culture that encourage intimate friendships between people of the opposite sex. How can you avoid some of those?

6. Do you believe you are vulnerable and therefore need hedges?

7. If your husband or wife realized they were attracted to another person, would you want them to talk to you about

it? Could you discuss it without feeling threatened and angry?

8. Mona and Gary described creating hedges for the eyes, the actions, and the mind. Share what each of these may look like practically in your opinion. Which is the one you struggle with most?

9. First Corinthians 6:18 instructs us to flee from sexual immorality. If you are the infidel, can you identify the point when you should have fled?

10. Read James 1:13–15. Talk about each step he describes.

12
Emotional Affairs

Anyone who even looks at a woman with lust has
already committed adultery with her in his heart.

Matthew 5:28 (NLT)

A book coming alongside couples in adultery recovery would be incomplete without addressing emotional affairs. So, not having experienced this ourselves, we want to share with you the stories of two couples who went through an emotional affair so you can have a glimpse into the reality of its beginnings, its effects, and its consequences. Both "Mike and Marie" and "Matt and Rachael" are real couples and their stories are true, but we have changed their names and some insignificant details to protect their privacy.

MIKE'S STORY

Mike was making his way to the lunchroom when he saw Sharon heading in the same direction. It seemed perfectly natural to ask if she wanted to join him.

"Sure, Mike, I'd love to!"

They settled in at a table and started discussing work. It wasn't more than five minutes before they were interrupted by someone who needed to talk to Sharon.

Mike let his thoughts wander. He felt proud his friend was a good employee. Sharon had quickly fit right in with the staff. She was fun to be around and did a great job.

When Mike and his wife, Marie, found out Sharon had gotten the job at the school where Mike worked, they'd been delighted. In fact, the two families had celebrated with a big backyard barbeque. Sharon, her husband, Ron, and their kids got together with Mike and Marie's family at least twice a week. They had fun together. They enjoyed a lot of the same things. Both families attended the same neighborhood church—in fact that's where they met.

Marie and Sharon had become best friends over the last year or so. Marie even commented that maybe a little of Sharon's "spiritual maturity" might rub off on Mike.

Mike had smiled and tried to ignore the sting those words had caused.

♥

"So how'd you think the new skit worked?"

Mike heard Sharon's question and realized he hadn't been listening. "What?"

"Where were you? The new skit we did at church on Sunday—how did you think it worked?"

Mike and Sharon had recently begun serving in the children's ministry at their church. The kids loved what they were doing, and it was very successful.

Mike was just glad he was finally beginning to feel like he belonged there. Church had always been a big issue between him and Marie. She'd been raised in a particular denomination, and her family was extremely loyal. Mike had known that before they'd gotten married. In fact, he had switched to her denomination because it didn't matter to him. But as time went on, he'd realized it did matter. Truth be told, he resented having to go to "her" church. Even after attending her family church for many years, he never felt like he belonged there. He couldn't appreciate all the traditions Marie and her family so loved. He wished they could be at a church that was "theirs."

Mike and Marie had been happily married now for sixteen years. Three great kids and a good life overall. Mike's career was on track. Marie was a wonderful wife and mother. They were a good fit. They communicated well—when they agreed. When they didn't agree, they usually just let it go.

Like the church thing. Mike had tried to explain to Marie how he felt. But Marie had told him, "Mike, it would be like cutting off my right arm."

There was just no winning on this one. So he let it go.

Then their middle daughter got involved with the neighbor kids in a nearby church, and she'd started working on her mom too. Mike wasn't sure why Marie had changed her mind, but the family had started attending the new church together.

They'd met Sharon and Ron in Sunday school. Sharon played a big role in helping Mike and Marie feel comfortable.

But Marie never seemed to find comfort there. In fact, she refused to become a member. Mike had been angry about that. He so wanted to be an insider rather than an outsider. But Marie had prevailed. She was already a member of a church—her childhood church.

Mike was just glad Sharon had invited him to serve with her in the children's ministry. He felt like he belonged there.

Mike and Sharon agreed on almost everything. She respected him and it showed. She was interested in what he had to say. She listened intently to his ideas for the children's ministry.

Unlike Marie. Marie was a real take-charge kind of woman. If there was a decision that needed to be made, she made it. Decisions came easily, with or without Mike's involvement. He just hadn't realized how much he enjoyed and wanted to be a part of the process.

Sometimes it bothered Mike that Marie didn't seem to need his input. His mom had done that too. The way she treated his dad had created resentment in Mike. And it had bothered him that his dad allowed it. Mom was cold and domineering and made every decision. At least Marie wasn't *that* bad.

♥

Mike and Sharon sat in the lunchroom talking about school, the ministry they shared, their families, and life in general. After lunch, he wondered briefly if he should be comparing her and Marie. Maybe he shouldn't enjoy these one-on-one lunches so much. He rationalized it as no big deal.

Three months later, lunch together every day had become a welcome routine for Mike and Sharon. They'd gravitated to eating in a room very few used. Very open, yet very private. No one could ever say they did anything wrong. Every day they shared more with each other. They talked about the kids, the challenges of trying to juggle life and all of its responsibilities. They talked about trivial things and things of great importance. And they began to share about the deficits they each saw in their spouses.

"If only Ron were more like you, Mike."

"Sharon, I so appreciate the way you listen to every suggestion I make and then we think things through together. Marie doesn't seem to care much about what I think."

One day another step in their relationship was taken. After sharing deep and intimate thoughts, Sharon reached across the table to touch Mike's arm. Mike's hand met hers halfway and their hands touched. It had been intended as simply a human touch to convey care and concern, but it became much more. Instead of pulling back, they both allowed their hands to linger. They smiled. Their eyes held. Then each looked away, slowly pulled their hand back, and began to gather their things. Lunch was over.

They got up and headed back to their offices. But this time separately. Something had just happened. They didn't know exactly what, but something had happened that day.

Lunch was never long enough anymore. And it had become the highlight of their day. The weekends seemed to drag by for Mike now. Even when the families got together, it just didn't feel the same, and he looked forward to spending those special lunchtimes with Sharon alone.

But it's only a very good friendship. It's only lunch. It's really no big deal. Really!

Fall turned to winter and soon the holidays were here. Mike and Sharon both felt kind of sad when the school break arrived.

New Year's Eve was going to be a blast. Several of the families at church were getting together to have a great evening of Christian fellowship while bringing in the New Year. The guys were off solving the world's problems while the girls were just talking and playing a card game at the huge dining-room table. Their uncontrollable laughter could be heard throughout the entire house.

Near midnight, the kids ran in yelling, "The ball is starting to drop. Come on, everybody!"

So everyone went into the family room, where the TV was on, showing the crowds out by the tens of thousands in Times Square. Mike could see Marie standing with the kids on the other side of the crowded room.

"10-9-8-7-6-5-4-3-2-1 ... Happy New Year!"

Mike was cheering with all his friends, but he didn't go over to Marie. He tried to convince himself that it just happened because one friend after another came up to shake his hand and before he knew it the moment had passed. As a couple, it was a tradition to bring in the New Year with a kiss. But Mike avoided Marie that year. Sharon was in the room. And that made it extremely uncomfortable.

Life went on. Winter became spring and the school year was ending. Mike knew the lunches would be ending too. And there was no denying now that their friendship had deepened into something very special. For the first time he wasn't looking forward to the end of the school year.

MARIE'S STORY

Marie saw Sharon's car pull up in front of the house through the dining-room window. Grabbing her purse and her list, she headed to the front door to join her best friend. She was glad that Sharon had agreed to go shopping with her for the end-of-the-school-year party.

Life was good. The kids were doing well in school. Mike's career was moving right along. They had good Christian friends. Even acquiescing to Mike and the kid's requests to start attending the neighborhood church had turned out well. Even though she did miss the traditions of her old church.

Mike had been a bit distant lately, and the phrase "midlife crisis" had crossed her mind. She tried to be a good wife and mother. And she was proud of the family she so diligently cared for. She smoothed down a stray hair, walked out the front door, and locked it.

She was glad she and Sharon could enjoy a few hours together before the kids got out of school and Mike got home.

Marie opened the car door and slid in. "How was your appointment?" The words were barely out of her mouth before she sensed something was wrong. One look at Sharon, and she knew she was right. Sharon stared straight out the front window. Had she been crying?

"What's wrong?" Marie's concern was audible.

"Marie, I have to tell you something." Then Sharon turned her head and looked into Marie's eyes.

Why did it suddenly feel like she knew what Sharon was going to say?

Don't say it, Sharon. Don't change everything. Don't ruin it.

It is amazing what effect the combination of fear and anger can have on your body. While the rest of her, including her heart, felt like it was taking a free fall off a bridge, Marie's back stiffened and she stared directly into the face of the woman next to her.

Sharon's eyes filled with tears and her shoulders slumped. "Mike and I, we …"

How dare you put your names together in the same sentence!

"Mike and I have gotten really close."

"Just what does that mean, Sharon? Has he touched you?"

"On my hand. Just my hand, I swear to you."

"Has he hugged you?"

Sharon's pause was answer enough. There was really no need for more words.

Marie's hand gripped the door handle. She had to get out of the car.

"Marie, please wait."

Sharon's impassioned plea did nothing to penetrate the separation that was now so tangible between them.

"Marie, please. You're my friend. I don't want to lose you. Please, can't we work through this? Can't we still be friends?"

Marie didn't recognize the voice that answered Sharon's question. "I don't think so." She opened the door and stepped out onto the sidewalk.

As she walked toward the front door, it seemed the world around her had taken on a surreal appearance. Everything looked the same. Nothing was the same. It would never be again.

She grabbed the door handle to let herself in the house. It was then that the first tear fell down her cheek. After several attempts with her shaking hand, the key went into the lock and the door opened, allowing her retreat.

What do I do now? How can I protect my family? Oh, God, how can I fix this? No one can know how badly I've failed.

She collapsed into the nearest chair. Some part of her heard Sharon's car drive away, but what did it matter now? How could she have been so stupid?

Her rambling thoughts settled on the party they'd attended for New Year's Eve just a few short months ago. She'd known then something was wrong. She'd felt it as distinctly as she was feeling it now.

Mike hadn't come to her. Not shared with her that first kiss of the New Year. She'd known then that she was no longer his best friend, and the stab of pain at that realization almost doubled her over.

Had he embraced Sharon that night? She couldn't remember.

But she remembered it was the first time they hadn't shared that kiss in sixteen years.

She didn't know how long she'd sat in the chair. But she did know when the clock struck three. The kids would be home soon. She was, after all, still a mother. And never before had her mothering instincts been more acute. No matter what, this would not be allowed to harm her children. She knew she had to stay, had to be what she was: a mother. Gainfully unemployed. All she knew was how to be a wife and—no, scratch that—a mother. And God help anyone who even thought for a moment she wouldn't protect her family with everything she had.

How she got through the next few hours she'd never understand. Somehow, she'd raised herself from that chair, hidden her tear-stained face and broken heart, and gone on with her duties. Even when Mike came home, she'd been able to pull it off. Until the kids went to bed.

"Michael, I know about you and Sharon."

"What? Me and Sharon? What are you talking about?"

"Michael, don't lie to me. Sharon told me you two have … gotten too close." It was an effort to even say the words, and once she did, the tears returned and whatever protective covering she had used to guard her children fell away. Pain made her grab her chest and sink down onto the bed.

"Marie, nothing happened between Sharon and me. You're making a big deal out of nothing. Honest, you have to believe me." Mike's voice communicated more than his words.

"Michael, she *told* me." Marie sobbed. "I saw it in her face."

"Marie, look at me." Mike took Marie's face in his hands and turned it toward him. "Honey, maybe we did get too friendly, but I swear to you nothing happened. And nothing will happen either. It's no big deal, really."

Marie pulled her face away from his hands. After a brief conversation, Marie ended it by saying, "Okay, Michael. But that woman and I—and you—are no longer friends. Do you understand me? We are no longer friends with her. I won't allow that woman to harm my family."

Marie's tone left no room for argument and Mike knew that from experience. He nodded his head in agreement. "Marie, I'm so sorry."

That day ended an era. The time when Marie thought she could easily keep her family safe. She would have to be a lot more careful now.

Over the next few months, things settled into another routine. The school year ended. Sharon would not be working at the same school next year. The kids hadn't asked too many questions, and it had been relatively easy to guide them toward other activities and friendships. Mike and Marie stopped attending their neighborhood church and followed some old friends to another.

Marie got many compliments on her recent weight loss. Food just didn't taste good and it was summer—"too hot to eat." She knew somehow she'd fallen off that pedestal Mike had always seemed to place her on. She didn't know how, and she didn't know why, but she'd do everything she could to climb back on. She learned to ignore the awareness that at times felt like something wedged between them. She missed him sometimes. It was just this midlife crisis thing and Mike would get over that and everything would be okay again. So she focused on her children and gave herself wholeheartedly to them.

After all, nothing had really happened.

MIKE AND MARIE

Mike and Marie went on about their lives after the "incident" with Sharon. They were young and busy. Marie focused her anger on Sharon and internalized all her fears about Mike. Neither of them wanted to explore what had happened. They didn't call it an "affair" until much later.

Thirteen years later, during an extremely stressful time in their lives, Mike had a physical affair with another woman he worked with. This time Marie's anger outweighed her fear, and they sought help. Marie says, "The emotional affair broke my heart. The physical affair broke our relationship."

When asked "What was your biggest mistake in dealing with the emotional affair?" Mike and Marie both agree they never healed at all. Marie didn't want to hear about it, and Mike really didn't want to talk about it, so they didn't. Both believe that because they didn't deal with the issues and do the hard work to repair their relationship, it left them vulnerable to another affair many years later.

When Marie learned about the emotional affair, she'd been fearful about how she could go on if Mike left her. Fearful about what everyone else would think. She would do anything to keep from looking like a failure as a wife and mother. So she just stuffed all the feelings way down deep inside, painted a plastic smile on her face, and went on with life. She tried to convince herself nothing ever "really happened," but in her heart she always knew that something had indeed happened. Something very big.

Mike, on the other hand, admits that he probably wouldn't have stopped the emotional affair on his own if Sharon hadn't confessed to Marie. Mike never believed that he had a problem in this area. He'd been strong. They never had sex. He really thought it was no big deal—at the time.

We asked Mike where, in retrospect, he had crossed the line in his relationship with Sharon. He told us two things:

When he began to look forward to their time alone together.

When he stopped sharing with Marie all that was being shared between him and Sharon.

When asked what they would share with couples going through the recovery of an emotional affair, they both passionately expressed to us:

"First, don't let big issues go unresolved. It may not be fun to find an answer you can both live with, but not dealing with that issue about the church left a weak spot in our marriage. A friendship with the wrong person at the wrong time found that weak spot."

"Secondly, when we realized the friendship had grown into something more, we denied it. Don't minimize it! Just because it isn't sexual doesn't mean it isn't an affair, and you need to deal with it. IT IS A BIG DEAL!"

♥

Mike and Marie did heal their marriage after the second affair. They got help and did the hard work. They were one of the first couples to participate in a Hope & Healing support group. They are over ten years post-affair recovery and serve as Hope & Healing facilitators. Mike and Marie also serve in their local church and now have eight beautiful and much-loved grandchildren. Both gratefully acknowledge that their time as grandparents would look quite different and they'd be missing something very special if they hadn't done the hard work of recovery.

RACHAEL'S STORY

Matt and Rachael were high school sweethearts—in between break-ups. It seemed Matt couldn't deal with a girlfriend and a team sport at the same time.

When they went for premarital counseling, the pastor told them there were some serious issues that had shown up on their respective tests and he was truly concerned. Rachael remembers Matt leaning forward and saying, "Pastor, we're getting married. Do you want to continue counseling us or do we need to go somewhere else?" Rachael had been in total agreement.

Seven years later Rachael and Matt had three children. Matt felt called to ministry rather than the family business. Rachael was a homemaker and mom. It should have been a sitcom from the fifties.

But it wasn't.

Somewhere along the road Rachael realized she'd been abandoned. Matt was busy with his ministry, and she felt as though she bore the entire burden for their family. Rachael felt she'd been transported back in time to the days when she and Matt broke up because he couldn't handle his team and his girlfriend. Only now the team had been replaced with the church. Their life had disintegrated into a routine where Rachael's role could have been performed by a paid employee. She felt alone. Where does a pastor's wife go when she knows there's trouble in her marriage?

She went to Matt. She tried talking, conveying her heart. She tried writing a letter detailing her concerns and expressing her feelings. Matt heard every word as a criticism, and they never were able to move beyond that. Her concerns went unheard. His concern was that his wife didn't love him unconditionally. After a few years and numerous attempts, it had culminated in a conversation where Rachael expressed her emotional bankruptcy by saying, "I don't love you anymore."

Instead of spurring either one of them into action, they both resigned themselves. She to a loveless marriage. He to … Rachael's thought ended there. She didn't know what he thought or planned. Did he even realize what had happened?

Maybe he hoped for a change when they moved to another state so he could attend Bible college. Maybe a little hope developed in her too. A new life. On their own without extended family.

So they settled into a new home. Matt started classes as a full-time student and accepted a position as the worship leader at their new church. Rachael enrolled in a couple of classes at the Bible college. She knew this would be a busy time, but she was in agreement with the plan to obtain Matt's degree and pursue a career in the ministry.

What she hadn't expected was that as the children grew older and wanted Daddy's time, Matt wouldn't give them priority any more than he had her. But Rachael resigned herself to getting through these couple of years. Surely it would get better … later.

Rachael turned her thoughts back to the Thanksgiving preparations. This would be the first time she'd prepared the meal by herself. Their friends Dennis and Linda were coming. All of them were students at the Bible college, and Dennis also served on the worship team.

She thought about the previous night at worship practice. She'd asked Matt a question, which he'd not answered. Then Dennis had looked her way, caught her eye, smiled, and mouthed the answer to her question. It felt so good to be heard. To be acknowledged as a person.

Thanksgiving dinner turned out well and everyone enjoyed it. After the meal they all went to the living room to sit down, and Rachael started clearing the table. She was exhausted. It caught her by surprise when Dennis came in and began helping.

Matt never did that.

Dennis and Rachael enjoyed the camaraderie of working together, and she realized just how much the kind act of helping meant to her. How hungry she was for male companionship. Dennis thought about her. Dennis made it fun. A part of Rachael began to blossom, and she thought for the first time that Dennis was an attractive man.

Rachael began enjoying even more any opportunity to spend time with Dennis after that. And it almost seemed as if someone, or something, was orchestrating that they run into each other. They found themselves at the same places and it wasn't planned. Surprise at seeing each other turned into enjoying each other's company without their spouses.

Smiles became private conversations.

Private conversations became casual and friendly touches.

Casual and friendly touches became the spark they both felt, and that spark had translated into intimate conversations about a future together.

Had Thanksgiving been only five months ago? How could life have changed so quickly? Within those five short months she and Dennis acknowledged their marriages were equally dead. Neither wanted this to happen. It just did. And as Christians they did what they believed was the correct thing. They did not fall sexually. They remained "faithful" to their respective spouses. That had to count for something.

Rachael confessed to Matt soon after realizing what had happened between her and Dennis. She was honest and admitted she had fallen in love with Dennis. They would be married and go on to serve together in ministry. Rachael knew Matt would be fine, and as a single dad he would by necessity be more involved with the children.

And Rachael could love and be loved.

MATT'S STORY

Matt woke from a sound sleep in the middle of the night sensing something was wrong. He realized Rachael wasn't in bed. The house was quiet and still.

"Rachael? Where are you?"

"Rachael!"

There was still no answer.

He made his way across the house, checking each room until he came to the spare bedroom. He could see the outline of her lying on the bed in the dark.

Matt turned the light on, wondering why she was there and not in their bed. Then his question changed as he took in her swollen eyes and noted the damp spot on the pillow.

"Rachael, what's wrong?"

She took a deep breath and opened her mouth as if to speak, but no words came. Her voice cracked and then she broke into uncontrollable sobbing.

Matt sat on the edge of the bed knowing something awful had happened. He reached to hold her and she pushed him back.

"I have to tell you something." Her words sounded as tortured as she appeared to be.

Matt felt terror rising from deep within him. The adrenaline rushing through his body washed any sleepiness away. "What is it, Rachael?"

"I told you a long time ago I wasn't in love with you anymore. But now I've fallen in love with Dennis."

Matt sat there with his eyes wide open, wishing it was a nightmare.

"You and Dennis? My best friend, Dennis? The guy I played handball with the other day?"

Rachael stared at Matt, sobbing and nodding her head.

Matt rose slowly from the bed. He could hear his heart pounding in his ears. As he walked out of the room, he turned the lights off.

Rachael stayed in the spare room.

By the time Rachael got home from taking the kids to school the next morning, Matt had a plan. They would go see Dennis and his wife. The four of them would discuss this, and the relationship would end. As a pastor Matt knew the right thing to do. And he was confident Rachael did too.

They were Christians. He'd soon be done with Bible college and was certain he'd be on staff at a big church within a few years. This was not going to change their plans.

The meeting with Dennis and his wife didn't go as Matt had anticipated. All the right words were spoken. Rachael and Dennis both claimed it hadn't gotten physical between them—there had not been a sexual affair. Then they'd all agreed Dennis and Rachael would not see each other again.

Matt knew he should feel relieved. But he didn't.

The following days were surreal. Matt felt uneasy.

Rachael was distant.

He thought about talking with her, but he didn't know what to say.

The invasive shrill of the phone ringing woke Matt and Rachael at two in the morning a few nights later.

Matt shot up in bed. "Hello?" He waited for a response. "Hello?" No one was there.

Rachael rolled over and groggily asked, "Who was it?"

"Wrong number I guess."

They both quickly fell back to sleep.

Matt woke again and glanced at the clock, which read 3:00 a.m. He reached over and felt only sheets and covers. Rachael was no longer in bed.

Terror shot through his entire body. He bolted out of bed and ran directly to the spare room, where he had found her before. Where she had confessed her love for Dennis.

She was not there either.

"Rachael?" Matt called into the dark house quietly enough not to wake the kids but loud enough to still evoke an answer. It took just minutes to search the entire house. She was gone.

Rachael, the perfect pastor's wife. How had this happened?

"Where is she, Lord? Is she with him? Has she left for good?"

Matt sobbed and held his head in his hands crying out to the Lord as the minutes turned into one hour, then into two hours. When he heard a key in the lock, it was 5:15 a.m.

"Where have you been?" Matt didn't even pause. "You've been with Dennis, haven't you? I can't believe this. What are you doing, Rachael? Have you gone crazy?"

The momentum of his anger grew. Matt was no longer the pastor. He had passed over into the raging husband.

He eventually paused long enough for Rachael to answer and confirm his suspicions. She'd been with Dennis.

Matt and Rachael began to talk about what was happening for the first time but had resolved nothing by the time the sun rose.

Matt knew he needed wise counsel, and he wanted to talk to his boss, the senior pastor of their church. He called and made an appointment to meet first thing that morning.

As he pulled into the parking lot, his head was still swimming from the events of the last few hours. He knocked on Pastor Robert's door.

A muffled "Come in, Matt" came from behind the door.

As he walked into the office, he collapsed into the chair directly across from Pastor Robert.

"You look terrible."

"It hasn't been the best night of my life." Matt paused. "Pastor, Rachael has been seeing—"

Pastor Robert cut him off. "I know all about it, Matt."

Matt's expression revealed his surprise.

"I was pulled aside a couple of Sundays ago and told of suspicions about Rachael and Dennis."

"You knew about this and didn't say anything to me?" Matt asked in disbelief.

"We didn't know what to do."

Matt stood up. "We?"

Pastor Robert crossed his arms over his chest and leaned back in his chair. "I had to take it to the elder board for a decision. We have to let you go."

"Let me go?" Matt shouted. He felt the blood drain from his head and wondered if he was going to pass out. "Let *me go?*"

"Now settle down, Matt. It was the only decision we could make. We can't have another scandal like the youth pastor caused. His affair about tore this church apart. You and Rachael can continue to attend the church, but I must ask that you keep this quiet. No one must know."

Pastor Robert continued, "Please have your letter of resignation, effective immediately, on my desk before you go home today. We will pay you through the end of the month, but please give me your keys now and clean out your office."

Matt had lost it all. It was too much to even begin to comprehend.

When he came home that night, Rachael informed him that she'd been asked to leave the Bible college.

Their lives were falling apart.

The harder Matt tried to save his marriage, the more his efforts seemed to push Rachael away. So he backed off and gave her the room she said she needed. It had been three months, and nothing had changed.

Matt had a part-time job teaching a class at the local college. He'd also been fortunate to get another job in town that would provide for his family's needs while they tried to figure out what the future held. Every time he left Rachael, he could feel his heart pound, and he constantly had to fight the panic that she would be gone when he got home. Tonight was no exception, and he forced his thoughts back to the students in the seats before him.

Out of the corner of his eye he saw someone looking through the window. He turned his head and realized it was Dennis's wife. She motioned for him to come out.

Not one part of him wanted to hear what she had to say. He was so weary.

After excusing himself, he went out. It was obvious she had been crying. "Matt, Dennis is still seeing Rachael. He's over at your house right now."

Matt ran to his car and skidded out of the parking lot, speeding through town like he was in a high-speed pursuit. In a sense he was.

When he burst through his front door, Dennis ran out the back.

Matt chased him through the backyard, over the fence into the neighbor's yard. The neighbor's dog went crazy, barking and biting at the men as it chased them through the yard. Dennis focused on escape. Matt focused on capture.

Dennis knocked the neighbor's gate open, ran across the front lawn, jumped into his car, and slammed it into gear. The tires screamed into the night.

As the tires' screeching faded, Matt heard Rachael screaming from the front porch, "Stop it, Matt!"

Matt walked back into his front yard.

"That's it. I'm through. I'm taking the kids and going back home. I'm done, Rachael. This is over. I just can't take it anymore."

Matt walked into what had once been his happy, perfect little home and began to pack.

He packed himself and all three children. He told Rachael they were going back home and invited her to come with them. Rachael stood there shaking her head, watching her life unravel before her, yet she was helpless to stop it. She couldn't go.

She watched Matt load the car. "Rachael, please come."

"I can't."

She watched Matt drive off.

MATT AND RACHAEL

Rachael sat on the couch and wondered if this was what she really wanted. Tears rolled down her already swollen eyes and onto reddened cheeks. She felt the roughness of the paper towel on her skin as she wiped the moisture from her chin and nose. Tissues couldn't keep up with the flow.

Oh, Lord, how did I get here? I have served You with my heart and my talents.

Fresh tears flowed again. *My God, what have I done?*

The shrill ring of the telephone interrupted Rachael's thoughts. A deep sigh escaped her lips. She knew it was Matt on the other end of that phone. Again.

"Hello?"

"Rachael, please reconsider. Come with us. Let me come back and get you. Don't do this."

"I'm sorry, Matt. But I can't." She lowered the phone back into its cradle.

Grabbing fresh paper towels, she lay down on the sofa. She was so tired. She felt much older than her twenty-nine years. *God, I obeyed You all my life. I was the good girl. I followed all the rules. Why didn't that—why didn't You—protect me?*

Rachael cried herself into an uncomfortable twilight sleep. Too tired to actually rest, too spent to do anything else. Images floated in and out of her dreamlike state. Dennis smiling and reaching his hand out to her. Her children's faces. Matt angry. Matt disinterested. Matt with pain etched in his features. Her conflicting thoughts and emotions would not allow her to fall into a deep sleep. Could she not escape even for a few hours?

You can't do this.

Rachael jerked up into a sitting position. Had she heard that or felt it?

You can't do this.

She knew there had been no audible voice. She also knew it was not her voice—audible or silent. She knew the source of those words.

You can't do this.

But I don't love Matt and I can't pretend I do.

You can't do this.

But I love Dennis. Can't I have this chance at love?

You can't do this.

Rachael sat and offered every argument she could think of. Every rationalization she knew. Every bit of hope she clung to. Yet the words never changed.

You can't do this.

Eventually Rachael ran out of words. Ran out of pleadings. Ran out of excuses. Until she could only hear those four words.

You can't do this.

Resignation settled inside her. Deeply. She didn't have a clue what would happen. She didn't even have any hope. But she could not deny the truth of those four words.

She couldn't do this.

It had been twelve hours since Matt left. He'd be halfway home now. When the phone rang again, she knew what she had to do.

"Hello?"

"Rachael, please come home with us? Please?"

"Matt, I don't love you anymore. You know that?"

"I know."

"If you'll accept me back knowing that truth, then I'll come home with you."

♥

Three more days would pass before Matt made it back over three states to pick up Rachael. She had some time to think and some more time to listen to God.

When Matt got there, Rachael explained she knew that God wanted her with her family so she would go back home and try to rebuild out of obedience to the Lord.

It would be a long time before Rachael understood why Matt came back. And even longer before she was glad she made the choice to go home. It was not easy. She told us the first year was the worst. In many ways Rachael went through a grieving process and declared Dennis dead—at least to her heart.

She and Matt were in counseling for a couple of years with a Christian counselor who helped them discover many areas in their relationship that needed attention. Matt saw for the first time that he had been having an affair as well. With his career. The church had become Matt's other woman.

So when it came time for Matt to find work, the church was out. He did menial jobs to pay the bills. Matt's most vivid memory is pushing a lawn mower, sweat pouring down his face, crying out to the Lord: "Father, I know You have called me into the ministry and yet You have me here. Mowing lawns? Why, Lord? Why?" Looking back, he knows this was a period of brokenness that could never be replaced. God had to humble Matt in a way that could allow him to see the man he had become.

We asked Rachael where, in retrospect, she had crossed the line in her relationship with Dennis.

. She told us, "When I got the 'tingles.' It sounds so ridiculous now, but at the time I believed since God's best plan—my marriage to Matt—was 'dead,' the relationship with Dennis was God's second-best plan. It was such a good feeling and I was so starved that it seemed impossible to turn away. My biggest mistake was to believe the lie that because I hurt so badly, sinful solutions were acceptable."

When asked what they would share with couples going through the recovery of an emotional affair, they both passionately expressed to us, "Prioritize yourselves as a couple. Learn to be friends. The time, effort, and money for counseling that our recovery required was worth it." Matt said he had to give Rachael time to realize he was changing his priorities. Rachael said she had to be obedient to God and open her heart before feelings for Matt turned into love again. It felt risky and scary to them both.

Matt would advise pastors to run into accountability, say with another pastor or counselor. Focus on the Family has an entire ministry devoted to pastors and pastors' wives, and it is completely confidential.

What did they learn through all this?

Rachael says her biggest lesson was how patient God is with us and how He continues to love us even when we've totally screwed up. He never gave up on her. "I gained a new understanding of 'blessed are those who mourn' once I finally came to the point of mourning my sinful behavior."

She also says she now is on guard and realizes how the Enemy takes advantage of our weakest areas. "If there is ever a moment or thought about a 'tingle,' even a dream, I immediately turn my thoughts over to God and ask Him to guard me and keep me holy. I'm willing to miss out on a friendship to prevent any chance of damaging my marriage or my relationship with God." Her advice to anyone tempted is simple: RUN.

Matt says he learned through this that God is sovereign. "I wanted to be married. I wanted to be a pastor. I wanted the perfect family. I wanted to be in control at all times. I wanted to make sure it happened."

♥

It's been over fifteen years, and Rachael and Matt did rebuild their marriage. There is love and there is trust. They share a grandchild. And they share a ministry. Matt is a pastor again serving in a large church. It doesn't look like Rachael thought it would look on that night so long ago, but she did get what she longed for. And Matt did too.

THE STORY ON EMOTIONAL AFFAIRS

The first time a couple contacted us about an emotional affair, it seemed like a lighter load to us than a physical affair—and that came across. Everyone agreed it was a betrayal of the marriage vows. But we were early in our recovery at the time and ignorantly believed that because the unfaithfulness had been revealed prior to a sexual encounter, the injury was less severe. We failed to comprehend then that the pain of that betrayal was just as significant to their relationship as that of a physical affair. The pain, loss, and grief of betrayal may be experienced from different causes, but it is not measured in increments. We will endeavor never again to underrate the pain another is feeling.

When God described marriage in the very beginning of time, He made it clear that the marriage relationship between husband and wife was to be the number one human relationship from that moment on: a one-of-a-kind, *intimate* human relationship.

The problem is not that we as human beings can *care* about more than one person; rather it's about what we *share* with another person.

The debate over whether or not men and women can be friends will probably never be decided to everyone's satisfaction. However, we believe if you add one word, *intimate,* then the decision has already been made. *Intimate* implies closely connected, personal, and confidential.

Dr. Shirley Glass says that "infidelity is that you took something that was supposed to be mine, which is sexual or emotional intimacy, and you gave it to somebody else."[1]

Plainly stated, *affairs are more about betrayal than about sex.*

The consequences of adultery will be different in every situation. But we have sat with too many spouses devastated by an emotional betrayal to not comprehend the depth of the pain. And in fact, it is not uncommon to hear a spouse say they can forgive the sex of a physical affair but the struggle is dealing with the emotional entanglement. That betrayal is the bigger wound.

So how can you tell if a friendship is crossing over the line into an emotional affair? We'll look to Dr. Glass again for three elements she considers necessary to determine whether a relationship is an affair: secrecy, emotional intimacy, and sexual chemistry.[2]

Secrecy

When attempts are made to hide feelings or actions in a friendship, something else is happening. You're enjoying it, but it's not something you want to share with your spouse—in fact it could be embarrassing or cause trouble. It's not always that your spouse doesn't know anything about your friendship. Marie knew about Mike's friendship with his coworker. But neither Mike nor Sharon told her what was happening at those lunches—that their friendship was growing, deepening, and becoming something they both looked forward to each day. *Secrecy is a testimony that you know you're doing something questionable.*

Emotional Intimacy

In an emotional affair you invest more emotional energy outside your marriage than in it and receive more emotional support and companionship from the new relationship than from your spouse. When you start confiding in your friend things you're reluctant or even resistant to share with your spouse, that's an indicator the emotional intimacy is greater in the friendship than in the marriage. When something happens and you think about sharing with your friend before you think about sharing with your spouse, that's another indicator you've invited someone to stand between you and your spouse. One of the best indicators of this increasing intimacy is sharing with your friend about the problems you're having in your marriage, as we saw with Rachael and Dennis.

Sexual Chemistry

Sexual chemistry is that subtle undercurrent of the awareness that this person is attractive to you. Author and speaker Gary Chapman calls it the "tingles." The truth is God created us to be sexually attracted to others—there is no sin in that occurring. But it is an indicator we need to limit contact with the person who elicits those tingles—unless we're married to them. And most therapists agree that this attraction is inflamed by its admission even if that admission is accompanied by a declaration that you will not act on it. In our case, Gary's partner admitted she "had to be careful around him" long before their affair became physical. The problem was that neither Gary nor his partner realized the power that chemistry had to feed the intimacy they were developing in their friendship. There is a reason that God advises us to "flee" sexual immorality (see 1 Corinthians 6:18 and 2 Timothy 2:22) rather than stand and fight to overcome those natural desires.

♥

The combination of secrecy, emotional intimacy, and sexual chemistry is a potent recipe that feeds an attraction. You are standing in quicksand, and if you fail to run, before you know it, you'll be up to your nose and in imminent peril of severely damaging your marriage.

So how does a person with no intention of ever betraying their spouse get into an emotional affair? The answer is very simple. You don't run when you should. You think you're above the temptation, or you think the person you're attracted to is above the temptation, and you just follow your natural instincts. You listen to the world tell you that nothing wrong is going on and that it's okay to have this friendship. You allow, maybe even manipulate, opportunities to be alone with this person. Slowly you build a relationship. You become so comfortable with a person of the opposite gender that you let your guard down and electricity fills the air. Then you find yourself preparing for those meetings like a teenager for a date.

The problem is that if we define infidelity only by its sexual contact, we then can feel free to pursue relationships that offer the excitement of something new without crossing physical lines. Often spouses, on the other hand, have little difficulty discerning when a friendship they are witness to has turned intimate, and very often these relationships cause increasing conflict between husband and wife. An emotional affair is in competition with the marriage, and often the spouse can sense it.

In our culture, staying connected is almost too easy. Besides being extremely mobile and on the go, we have cell phones, email, text messaging, instant messaging, and social networking sites like Facebook. And with the aid of the Internet, these relationships can even begin with a total stranger. After all, it can feel "private" and even anonymous at first. If you're wondering about a relationship, take a look at who you're communicating with and how often. The electronic trail we leave can be pretty informative.

So what do you do if you find yourself in what could be termed an emotional affair? That same biblical advice we mentioned earlier still applies—run. Continuing the relationship will spell disaster for you and the person you're involved with.

The irony is that sometimes extracting yourself from an emotional affair can be even more difficult than from a physical affair, especially if you rationalize that *nothing has happened*. If you can see that an emotional affair has occurred, understand that your marriage has suffered a severe wound. Take the energy that has been invested in the illicit relationship and redirect it to the healing and strengthening of your marriage.

If feelings were acknowledged between you and your affair partner, the healing will look like the healing from an affair that was sexual. In fact, we believe that almost without exception, an emotional affair left to its own will become physical. Every principle we've talked about in this book applies to healing from an emotional affair.

However, even if the feelings haven't been verbalized between you and the affair partner, the fact remains that new boundaries need to be established.

We suggest that one of the first steps in extracting yourself out of an emotional affair is to come home and confess to your spouse. Some might think, *Wait a minute; this is one I don't need to confess because nothing really happened. It'll only upset my spouse and cause even more problems.* Unless there is a safety issue or something of that magnitude, we really do think bringing the truth out into the light is the best course of action. Explain to your spouse what has happened and the temptations you are now fighting, then enlist their help. This confession accomplishes three things.

First, just as we explained in the chapter on hedges, it diffuses the power of secrecy. The thrill of a shared secret has now become a threat to your family. And your fantasy world has been exposed to reality.

Second, it helps prevent escalation of the relationship. The steps you now take will prevent the relationship from progressing into something more.

Third, it is a great motivator to immediately end the relationship and begin working to rebuild your marriage with your spouse.

We encourage couples to discuss together and be in agreement with what steps will be taken to decrease or eliminate contact between the infidel and partner. Obviously, there will be no more private meetings. No more intimate conversations. The intimacy you were willingly giving to someone else belongs to your spouse.

Work situations that will continue to require contact with the affair partner will require more creative solutions, but it is still possible to eliminate the secrecy and emotional intimacy. We suggest all contact be professional—no personal exchanges at all. If the partner asks questions, the infidel should have a reply ready that they and their spouse have agreed to. Maybe something like "I've realized it is inappropriate to discuss my personal life with you. From now on we'll just focus on work-related subjects." End of discussion. And anytime there is contact with the partner, the infidel needs to tell their spouse as soon as possible.

The bottom line is that the couple focuses on their relationship, and the affair partner no longer is able to take energy away from that priority. And the possibility of offending your spouse overrides the possibility of offending the affair partner. True, if you follow our suggestions, the way you see yourself reflected in your affair partner's eyes may change, but that's a good thing. Better to be thought of as an honorable husband or wife than an attractive partner.

The question then remains: Can men and women have friends of the opposite sex? The answer in our opinion is yes. But here is the determining factor: That friend of the opposite sex needs to be a friend and a respecter of the marriage. Dr. Shirley Glass says, "They are not in competition with the marriage and reinforce the value of the marriage in general and their friends' commitment to that marriage in particular."[3]

We both have opposite-sex friends. But most of our time with those friends is spent as couples. And we do not go out alone with a friend of the opposite sex. Our friends may not agree with the hedges we have put in place, but as friends of the marriage, they will not entice either one of us to climb over them.

Working with your spouse to heal the damage an emotional affair has caused to your marriage is worth the effort it requires. Thomas Hardy, the author and poet, said, "New love is the brightest, and long love is the greatest, but revived love is the tenderest thing known on earth."[4]

We can only agree.

The following quizzes were developed by Dr. Shirley Glass. Taking the quiz and discussing the results with your spouse could lead to a very beneficial and interesting conversation. Be honest!

Has Your Friendship Become an Emotional Affair?

1. Do you confide more to your friend than to your spouse about how your day went? Yes No

2. Do you discuss negative feelings or intimate details about your marriage with your friend but not with your spouse? Yes No

3. Are you open with your spouse about the extent of your involvement with your friend? Yes No

4. Would you feel comfortable if your spouse heard your conversation with your friend? Yes No

5. Would you feel comfortable if your spouse saw a videotape of your meetings? Yes No

6. Are you aware of sexual tensions in this friendship? Yes No

7. Do you and your friend touch differently when you're alone than in front of others? Yes No

8. Are you in love with your friend? Yes No

Scoring Key:

You get one point for each yes to questions 1, 2, 6, 7, 8, and one point for each no to 3, 4, 5.

If you scored near 0, this is just a friendship. If you scored 3 or more, you may not be "just friends." If you scored 7–8, you are definitely involved in an emotional affair.

Is Your Online Friendship Too Friendly?

What are the warning signs that you (or your spouse) are on the slippery slope to an online affair? Take this online-relationship quiz and see.

1. Do you find yourself coming to bed later at night because you're chatting online? Yes No

2. Do you ever exit a screen because you do not want a family member to see what you are reading or writing to a chat-room member? Yes No

3. Have you ever lied to your spouse about your personal Internet activities? Yes No

4. Would you feel uncomfortable sharing your Internet correspondence with your spouse? Yes No

5. Have you ever set up a separate email account or credit card to carry on a personal correspondence with an individual online? Yes No

6. Has your Internet correspondence had a negative effect on your work or household tasks? Yes No

7. Have you ever lied in response to a question from your spouse about your email correspondence? Yes No

8. Have you ever exchanged photos of yourself with a secret email correspondent? Yes No

9. Since beginning a secret email correspondence, have you experienced either a loss of or an unusual increase in sexual desire for your spouse? Yes No

10. Have you made arrangements to talk secretly on the phone with your email correspondent? Yes No

11. Have you made arrangements to meet with your secret email correspondent? Yes No

Scoring Key:

Two or more yes answers to questions 1, 2, 3, 4 indicate a potential Internet romance is developing. It is time to either share your online correspondence with your mate or break off the correspondence and begin to examine how to improve your marriage.

A yes answer to any of questions 5, 6, 7 indicates you are crossing the boundary from an Internet friendship to an Internet romance. Acknowledge this relationship for what it is about to become and take action to preserve and enhance your marriage.

A yes answer to question 8 or 9 indicates you have begun a fantasy romantic relationship with your online correspondent. Even if it never moves to a physical stage, this relationship has great potential to damage or destroy your marriage.

A yes answer to question 10 or 11 indicates you have taken positive action toward initiating an extramarital affair. Consider the impact this will have on your marriage and your children and take steps to sort this out with a professional.

13

Healing Timeline from a Couple's Perspective

Behold, I will bring ... health
and healing, and I will heal
them; and I will reveal to them an
abundance of peace and truth.

Jeremiah 33:6 *(NASB)*

When *Unfaithful* was first written, we acknowledged that most of us want to know how long this recovery process will take. We shared the truth that "the length of your recovery cannot be predetermined—and most likely you both will be on different time schedules." And we intentionally avoided giving any sort of timeline because we didn't want anyone to measure their recovery against a time frame and wonder what was preventing them from fitting into it.

What we have come to understand since is there are some advantages to understanding the process from a perspective of time. Particularly when we hit a difficult period and can know that it's a common occurrence for others in recovery about that same time.

The longer we have worked with couples and heard their stories, the more we realize that those who come alongside these people often have a much different idea of the path recovery will take than what most couples experience. That alone creates tension for the couple.

In addition, as a society we're advocates of the instant fix. Serious problems are resolved within hours or, at the very most, weeks. And when they're not, it is often assumed it's because the problem is actually too big to be resolved or someone is not doing something right. This attitude does little to encourage a couple to persevere through the convoluted process of healing from infidelity.

So we have decided to share with you a recovery timeline. Before we begin, we must remind you that people do not fit perfectly into boxes or timelines. Relationships and individuals have too many variables, such as:

- Our individual marital histories
- A previous betrayal we've experienced
- Feelings and behaviors that are in response to memories, in addition to what is currently happening
- Coping skills that are influenced by those around us
- Cultural upbringing that affects our responses to crisis in general and infidelity in particular

The point is we do not claim this as an absolute but rather as a guide. With that being understood, let's take a look at the beginning of the process in a recovery timeline. Reference the table at the end of this chapter for summaries of these phases and the recovery timeline.

Phase 1: Revelation

The process of adultery recovery as a couple usually begins with revelation. Revelation is when the infidel admits to the spouse that an illicit relationship has occurred, either through confession or by being caught undeniably in a relationship. Even if a spouse has spent several days, weeks, or months being suspicious before the infidelity is confirmed, for this timeline "revelation" starts at that confirmation or admission.

What is most important to understand is that the *responses* or *expressions* to revelation are overwhelming and they are temporary. (That is not to say that the emotions or feelings are temporary but rather how they're expressed.) This is a shock, a trauma—an event so severe that many liken it to the response a person would have to the death of a loved one.

This is an overwhelming event, like being in the middle of the ocean and having wave after wave sweep over you. Because the shock and trauma are so severe, it makes sense that the person has difficulty thinking. They can't focus. They feel as though they're moving in slow motion. They can often have trouble understanding what's being said in whole but later will be able to repeat words or phrases verbatim. And any infidel who attempts to "rephrase" a revelation will encounter extreme reactions to any change in the story.

The emotional response is also physically overpowering. It's that picture of someone who literally can no longer stand on their own two feet. We'll talk about how that surprising response may look in a moment.

The infidel certainly is also experiencing a trauma, but it is different than the experience of the spouse at revelation. Commonly the infidel has almost a sense of relief. A double life takes effort and energy, and most infidels are exhausted. So once revelation has happened, relief can be experienced. It is not at all uncommon for an infidel to have a good night's sleep for the first time in a long while at the same time the spouse is unable to sleep at all.

After that intense emotional shock and trauma have subsided a bit, processing what's happened begins. You may still feel like you're in the middle of the ocean, but the waves have calmed and you're able to tread water—albeit weakly.

For the timeline, processing begins after *all* has been revealed. If the infidel confesses or admits only partial truths, allowing the spouse to believe that it is the full story, and then at a later time admits to more truth, revelation becomes a series of events rather than a onetime thing. We call this *serial revelation.*

Each new piece of information, each new admission, will put the spouse right back at revelation emotionally. And this is true whether it's been one day, one week, one month, or one year. So if there is any advice we could offer an infidel here it would be to *tell it all now.* Any untold truth that you attempt to hide, figuring it might never come out, is a weapon laid directly at Satan's feet. It's like needing four new tires and buying only three to save money: It just doesn't work. It is a weakened area that will not go away and in fact under the right circumstances can become more of a danger than it was before. If your motive is to save your spouse more pain, then speak all the truth from the beginning. Each time your spouse is thrown back to revelation, it increases their pain, increases the difficulty of your healing process, and will severely affect the rebuilding of trust.

So in those first few days, when your spouse comes and asks if there is anything more, tell whatever more there is. And do not attempt any further lies.

Phase 2: Approximately 0 to 6 Months after Revelation

Phase 2 begins when you start to work together as a couple: when you explore together what happened and how it happened and begin to deal with the thoughts and feelings you are both experiencing as a result of the infidelity. This phase can start immediately after revelation or several months after revelation. Why? Because if those first few months (or even longer in some cases) are spent trying to figure out what you want and what you are willing to do, phase 2 has not yet begun.

Many times we'll have couples come to us and say, "It's been almost a year and we haven't made any progress. We just don't think we can do it." Then we'll talk with them about what has and has not been happening during the past year. They admit they were on separate journeys for quite a while and haven't spent much of that time working together. Maybe the infidel left their spouse and lived with the partner for a few weeks or months, then "came to their senses" and returned ready to work for the first time. Maybe the spouse requested a separation because they just "couldn't do this." Perhaps neither of them could bring themselves to even discuss what had happened. Maybe it's been a Cold War atmosphere with skirmishes in which many hurtful things have been said and done in a battle zone that established itself between them.

That couple's processing began for this timeline when the two separate journeys came together and they began working toward a common goal: healing the marriage together and discussing what happened and how they might have gotten here.

Often when we've been able to share this concept with a couple, they can let go of how long it's been since revelation and they can get what we call "an infusion of hope." They realize that even though revelation may have been some time back, their processing and working on healing the marriage is relatively new. We can assure them that we have seen God do mighty things when both will work together no matter when they start processing.

Healing is a combination of time and working together. Time alone may decrease the intensity of emotions, but it does nothing for the work. Frankly, time without work doesn't count. And in fact it can lead to a false sense of healing. Working together can be productive, but time is required to absorb what has happened and how it feels.

Can a couple be separated and work together on this common goal of healing the marriage? We believe so, but we also think it is more difficult simply because your time spent together is greatly reduced. Those opportunities that just happen late at night or spontaneously in the middle of an ordinary activity are less likely to occur. So processing time has to be scheduled and both need to be much more intentional about doing the work of healing when they are together.

So is it a bad idea to separate? We couldn't make a blanket statement on an issue with so many convoluted edges. We do believe there are times separation is valid. Certainly if there are safety issues for either of you. And it's not uncommon for some to require time alone to comprehend what has happened. The point is that separation adds another dimension to the healing process.

Let's look at how some of the common responses to revelation look. Again, we don't claim to be therapists or experts; we're just sharing with you what we've frequently observed and had validated by the couples with whom we've worked. These responses begin with revelation and continue during phase 2.

Typical Spouse Responses

Whatever the primary emotional response to revelation is, it tends to be temporary. As you move into phase 2 and start working together, you'll see that emotional responses swing from one type to another. That's pretty standard for the situation you're in. Many times, especially during these first two phases, couples are most grateful for the assurance that they're probably not going crazy—rather they're responding to a very deep shock and trauma, and what they're experiencing is normal for the abnormal situation in which they find themselves. Most of us here are in uncharted territory and we really don't understand what's happening. We also find hope during this time to be elusive.

Responding with Anger

The spouse who responds with anger is probably the most common to us because they're the ones who are out there shouting it from the rooftops. This person tells everyone or insists that the infidel tell everyone. They are not concerned with who knows. And often this spouse will take advantage of any opportunity to convey just how awful the infidel has been—even to their children.

What we need to understand is that behind this loud and vocal anger is a hurt person trying to survive. A person crying out for help. This is self-preservation. In fact, there is a physiological response we have called "fight or flight." This is the body's response to a perceived threat or danger. During this reaction, certain physiological things occur that give the body a burst of energy and strength. In addition, there is another component of this response that suppresses pain. [1] The person whose response is anger is so overwhelmed they can't see beyond the ton of bricks that continues to fall and threaten. It is just too much.

If this was your primary response, you may need to go back later to some people and apologize for what you said or how you said it. If possible we suggest you go together as a couple. Convey that you're working together to try to heal the damage done to your marriage and you'd both appreciate their help. Some will want to know what they can do, so give them ideas. They can pray. They can watch your children so you have time alone together to do the processing. But encourage them to come alongside both of you as a couple rather than just the person who's been wounded. The point is to heal and rebuild the marriage.

What we encourage you not to do is avoid the subject. Just as a general rule of thumb, we suggest that as much of the pain as you have shared with others, that much of the healing process also needs to be shared with those same people. So if they witnessed the initial destruction, allow them to witness the rebuilding, too. If not, if all you've left them with is the pain and ugliness, then they'll have little to offer you in support, and that's unfair to everyone. The same holds true for your children.

Sin and pain affect everyone they touch. The anger is a normal and natural response to betrayal; the problems come in how we express that anger. Anger tells us something is wrong, so focus on what you can do about that. We shared some suggestions for processing that anger in chapter 8.

Responding with Fear

The spouse who responds with fear we don't often see because they're hiding. They're trying to figure out how they can do this without anyone finding out. And it's usually not going too well. It takes a lot of energy to act like everything is fine when you're dying inside. And it robs you of a lot of good support. We are often contacted by people who feel completely isolated because no one knows what has happened.

This person will have a diminished ability to continue with all the responsibilities they have, so they back away from things they used to enjoy. Most will continue to go to church, at least some of the time, because they don't want anyone to be too suspicious something is wrong. They'll shake your hand, smile, and respond, "I'm fine. How are you?" when greeted. If they've told anyone, it is a very select few and they have sworn those few to secrecy. They feel terribly alone because in many ways they are. The world keeps on turning and those around them continue with daily activities while they feel as though they are dying one small piece at a time. They see no light at the end of the tunnel but rather a tunnel that never ends.

If this is you, can we encourage you to reach out to someone who can help you through this? Professional counselors are bound by confidentiality laws, and all of us need godly counsel to work through this. The longer we try to do this alone, the more difficult it actually becomes. If counseling is not available locally, there are some intensives available out there—places where couples can go to receive intensive counseling for a few days. Don't rob yourselves of the opportunity to get the help you need or allow fear and shame to keep you isolated from resources that can help you heal.

Responding with Pain

The spouse who responds with pain is what we call the "walking wounded." They may look like they're doing okay from afar, but they're barely pulling that off. And if you look closely, they are dazed and confused. This is where Mona landed at revelation and wandered in and out of during much of our recovery. She searched to find someone who could understand what she was feeling, another couple who had been through adultery recovery and gotten through the pain. The pain was incapacitating, and she feared it would never be gone.

If we were to place a plaque over the door for a Hope & Healing support group meeting room, it would read "I Want My Life Back!" Those words have been uttered out of pain by many of the people we've worked with. It's taking all they have just to function and do what they have to do, and nothing seems to help. We often tell couples to think of themselves as if they'd been physically injured. There are many things we'd not try to accomplish if we were physically injured. We'd give ourselves some time to heal and ask others to take on what we couldn't do for a while. Permit yourselves to acknowledge an injury has occurred. Focus on what is necessary: eating correctly, getting rest, the essentials of parenting, the essentials of earning a living. Give yourself permission to take a break and work on healing. It may feel like nothing seems to help you right now but hold fast. The good news is that you can work through the pain and resume your life as the healing progresses.

You may have noted that these first three—anger, fear, and pain—are primarily the spouse's reaction to revelation. There is a reason for this. In his book *Torn Asunder,* Dave Carder says, "If you're the infidel ... even though you were in the driver's seat in initiating the affair, at this stage you're in the passenger seat."[2]

The point is that much of the infidel's behavior will be in *response* to the spouse's reaction to revelation. We believe if the infidel can comprehend what is going through the spouse's mind and heart, what is behind the behavior, they have a better opportunity to respond in ways that can benefit the healing process—whether or not they want to save the marriage at this point.

If you have children together, this person will continue to be a part of your life, and both of you need to heal from this injury to go on and be healthy parents. Even without children, you both need to heal or the issues that got you here will go with you into any future relationships—along with the unhealed wounds. And they'll still carry the power to cause damage.

Responding with Grace

If you as a couple have responded together with grace, we'll praise the Lord with you. Your experience at revelation found both of you looking to God and having almost a miraculous understanding of what happened. You are willing to get help and to heal together. Quite frankly, you look good, and pastors wish every couple who came to them had your experience. You're having intimate and deep talks like you never had before. You feel close to one another, and in fact couples often say, "This is the relationship we've been praying for."

We do know that God does miraculous things. But we also know that injuries this deep leave wounds, and wounds need to heal. Both of you will discover those wounds as time goes on and you begin processing. And most of the time, the Lord allows us to experience healing so we can learn from the process.

God does not waste pain, and this is one area where we often can see a gain at the other end. Neither of us are the same people we were before we went through the healing process to rebuild our marriage. And quite frankly, we're glad. We like ourselves and each other a whole lot more. Even though the situation of adultery recovery is steeped in sin, deception, and pain, God can and does bring benefit to each of us when we follow His lead. So we advise you not to miss the opportunity and to encourage one another to go through the process.

That initial grace can be a gift, but don't be surprised when the anger, fear, and pain come too as you walk down this road. It doesn't mean something is wrong; it means your heart and mind have caught up with each other. That initial shock is beginning to wear off and the processing is beginning. The same God who sat with you at revelation will walk with you through those emotions to the end of this healing journey and beyond.

♥

The things that happen at revelation and in those first few months of recovery have an enormous effect on us as individuals. There are some things those of us who go through this will never forget. But we want to make sure you hear this clearly. No matter what does or doesn't happen here at the beginning, processing what's happened still needs to occur and reconciliation is still possible.

These are extreme times and we often have intense responses to what's happening. But it is not over here. God does some of His best work after a mountaintop experience and after we've been in rebellion for a while. So whether you and your spouse have drawn together or polarized during this time, the end of your story is not written yet. In the timeline there is still plenty of opportunity for hope, and healing is indeed possible.

These first few months after revelation are commonly filled with many discussions. We've already shared with you how those conversations can help or hinder the process when we discussed talking in chapter 8. Often couples disagree on the benefit of these discussions, but for a time both acknowledge the necessity. Then they begin to experience some of the things we'll describe in phase 3.

PHASE 3: APPROXIMATELY 6 TO 12 MONTHS AFTER REVELATION

When this phase begins depends on when you began working together and how intensive the work has been. It is characterized by weariness. And when you try to see what progress has been made, it can be difficult to visualize from your perspective.

We have some new homes being built near us. It seemed to take forever to clear the land and get it ready. Finally, the framing began and we soon could see the positioning of walls. The trusses and roof went on. Things appeared to move quickly at this point: The windows went in, insulation was put in place, and the outside walls took shape. Then things seemed to slow down. We'd see workers but couldn't see any progress being made on the house. It was during this time that the work was being done *inside* those recently erected outside walls. We were unable to appreciate the progress from our perspective.

During this weariness phase in recovery, a similar situation occurs. You feel like you have been rebuilding a house. You are exhausted. The magnitude of the injury is understood.

In addition, life has begun to call both of you back as participants. Family, jobs, and those essentials you've been trying to cover these past weeks continue to call your name. You do the best you can. And some seem to pull it off. You can appear to be stable and functioning. But at night when you lie down, the exhaustion permeates every inch of your body. The healing of your relationship is not complete, and you're both very aware of this fact.

One of the most important aspects of healing during this time is the rebuilding of trust, which will require both of you working together. It is a slow process. It also will require transparent honesty from both of you. And it will require integrity, an undivided and unbroken adherence to the process of healing.

The irony is that this is often when our support begins to fade. The time between counseling sessions is extended if the counselor believes you're doing well or if your checkbook begins to run dry.

Those who have supported you, if you enlisted support in the first place, are also becoming weary. Those who watch someone they care about go through a painful time also experience pain themselves. And if your supporters are uninformed about adultery recovery and the depth of the healing process, you may begin to hear some different messages:

"You know, you've been working on this marriage diligently for (fill in the blank). I've watched you and (insert spouse's name) both work hard, and I've seen God work in both of you. Maybe it's time to just let it go. Accept God's healing and move on. There's nothing else either one of you can do and if you keep obsessing on this, it might turn out badly."

Or: "You have done everything you could to try to heal this marriage. God does allow divorce for adultery and maybe this is the reason why. Maybe it is just too hard. You deserve some happiness and I just can't stand to see you suffer anymore."

These words are more about what the speaker wants than they are about you. Adultery recovery is hard but it's not *too* hard. And God's plan for marriage—one man, one woman for a lifetime—doesn't change because of this sin. Neither does His plan for you as His child. You're weary because you've worked hard. That's normal for what you're going through.

There are two common temptations at this point. All of us in adultery recovery want the process to end; we want our lives back. To get there, you *must* walk all the way through the process—no quitting in the middle. If you quit, you only extend it or, worse yet, stop the process altogether and don't heal completely. Then when you or your marriage again comes under stress, those areas of incomplete healing will be weakened areas that are vulnerable. Quitting just isn't worth the risk.

The second temptation is to simply give up. Lose the hope you had for healing and resign yourself to the marriage you have as it is now. If you don't head straight for the divorce court, you may be able to pull that off for a while. Then it will begin to wear on you, you'll find yourself spiraling down, and you run the risk of becoming bitter or finding another way to cope with your unhappiness.

We want you to know there is another option. And that option is to heal. Healing takes time. The goal is a healthy marriage that you both cherish and that honors God. Don't miss this opportunity. Persevere. Do the hard work. It's worth it.

PHASE 4: APPROXIMATELY 1 TO 2 YEARS AFTER REVELATION

The emotional ups and downs will continue to occur, but you'll notice a decrease in their frequency, intensity, and duration. We encourage couples to keep their eyes on healing, keep the goal of a healthy marriage in sight. They'll still continue to process, but it will be more intermittent.

Then the "triggers" come.

What happens during phase 4 is very much like what happens when a death has occurred. Dates and anniversaries have new meanings and evoke many emotions. In a grieving process these reminders are often called "anniversary reactions." [3] And the reactions you experience may feel eerily like the emotions during phase 2 of the healing process. We'll call these reminders *triggers*.

When a marriage experiences infidelity, life is often broken down into three parts: the time before the affair, the time when the affair was ongoing, and the time since the affair ended. Spouses are even more acutely aware of these designations and feel a need to reevaluate everything that happened during each part. Mona questioned if anything before the affair was true and honorable. Obviously during the affair nothing was true or honorable, at least from her perspective. After the affair it was simply craziness.

Some spouses will go through their homes and eliminate anything that reminds them of the time during the affair. We encourage spouses who feel these reminders must be removed to box them up and store them somewhere safe. Do not destroy anything until you can think clearly again. If you still feel it must all go in a year or two, the box can be easily destroyed. But if you should change your mind about any of its contents, you'll have that option also.

Phase 4 often marks the arrival of unexpected reminders—*unexpected* because you thought you'd already dealt with things. Then you see something, hear something, smell something, read the news, watch a television program, any number of mundane activities, and suddenly you're flooded with emotions that cause you to feel as if you're reliving those initial responses all over again.

Then there are the obvious moments: the date of revelation, your birthday, a holiday—significant dates that remind you where you were last year on this day. There is no way to avoid these so we encourage you to acknowledge the elephant in the room. Bring it up. Talk about it. Grieve if you need to. Time will decrease the intensity of the sadness and emotions, but having them is normal. Don't let the Enemy lie to you and tell you that you're not healing if you have a response to a trigger.

One of our couples decided to handle the anniversary of revelation by making a new memory. They scheduled a rededication ceremony. It was small and included only their pastor, counselor, and Hope & Healing facilitators, but it was very meaningful. And from now on, if they feel sadness on that date, they can also experience joy in the memory of a special and private moment.

Trust continues to be rebuilt during this time. It is fragile and must still be handled with care. It will require time to mature and feel solid. It is also during this time that life seems to feel as though it's returned to normal. That can be unsettling, especially to the spouse. After many months of intensive time together it can almost feel as though distance has developed between you. That itself can bring about anxiety because feeling distanced from one another is often a hint there is something wrong.

Neither of you knows what normal looks like for you as a couple now. When do you know something needs intervention? What will be okay to disregard or overlook? Keeping all these questions exposed to the light, discussing them when they come up, and conveying your feelings and what brought them on will enable both of you to begin to grasp and become comfortable with your "new normal."

This is a good time to develop new habits together. Our cofounders discovered they enjoyed cooking together. They took a class. They experimented with recipes. Other couples have taken up a new hobby or sport. What you do isn't nearly as important as doing it together. Having fun together is also part of a healthy marriage.

We encourage you not to drop your support here. There will still be difficult moments, especially when the triggers arise. This is a good time to continue growing together spiritually. Reading some of those books that were recommended or taking a class with other couples can be very helpful, and often you're both ready to take intentional steps forward to nurture your relationship.

When is phase 4 over? When are you done with this healing process? The answer is simple really. It's over when you both say it's over and not a minute before. And the truth is that often it's not clear when that occurs, only that in retrospect it did.

Do the work. You can have love. You can have respect. You can have trust. We have heard it time and time again from the couples we have been blessed to work with. After the hard work of recovery they now enjoy a level of intimacy they never dreamed would be possible when they started the process. Enjoy the progress you make. This is an investment that can last and grow for a lifetime.

ADULTERY RECOVERY TIMELINE
From a couple's perspective

BEGINNING OF THE PROCESS	
PHASE 1	PHASE 2
REVELATION (can be serial)	0–6 MONTHS (time varies)
OVERWHELMING and TEMPORARY	VACILLATING BETWEEN RESPONSES
Shock, trauma, much like a death Often return here after "serial revelation" Difficulty thinking	Both working together Revelation complete Hard work begins
FIRST RESPONSES	*PROCESSING BEGINS*
Anger Tell everyone—scream from the rooftops Villainize the infidel Self-preservation	**Anger** "Fight or flight"—survival Cry for help Too much, I can't, I won't
Fear Hiding, withdrawal from normal activities "Smiling" at church Select few sworn to secrecy	**Fear** Terrified they can't heal—hopeless Shame is great Nobody knows—feel alone
Pain Walking wounded Dazed and confused Enlist a few for support	**Pain** Depression—"want my life back" Barely functioning Nothing seems to help
Grace United front "Seen the light" Willing to heal and get help Look good but not processing yet	**Grace** Intimate and deep talks Emotions (anger, fear, pain) will manifest Beginning to understand the work of processing

ADULTERY RECOVERY TIMELINE
From a couple's perspective

PROCESS CONTINUES	
PHASE 3	**PHASE 4**
6–12 MONTHS (time varies)	1–2 YEARS
WEARINESS	KEEPING YOUR EYES ON HEALING
Hard work continues Difficult to see progress	Keep working Ups and downs continue but are lessening
PROCESSING ONGOING	*PROCESSING INTERMITTENT*
Roller-coaster ride vs. real life Aware of magnitude of injury Exhausted May appear stable and be functioning	**Triggers** Before, during, after timelines Calendar dates/anniversaries Involuntary thoughts
Support eventually begins to fade Supporters weary too Mixed messages—"get over it" vs. "too hard" Counseling may end or decrease	**Redefining the marriage** "Normal" can feel frightening Rebuilt trust is fragile Agree on new rules—hedges
Temptation Quit working—"slide into old normal" Stop healing process and healing incomplete Give up—lose hope, stop healing process, and spiral down	**Develop together** New habits How to deal with future issues Continuing resources and support
Rebuilding trust Transparent honesty Slow process—onus on infidel, give spouse time	**When is the process over?** When both say it's over Enjoy the progress

Afterword

A Personal Letter to
You from Gary

Dear Reader,

I've just finished my quiet time. Today my devotional time centered on giving to others in need. The verse was Matthew 25:32, where Jesus divided the sheep and the goats: "All the nations will be gathered before him, and he will separate the people one from another as a shepherd separates the sheep from the goats."

All the nations will be gathered before Jesus as He sits on His throne in heavenly glory. Then will come the great division. Those to His right, blessed by His Father, will be summoned to take their inheritance—the kingdom prepared for them since the creation of the world. For when He was hungry, they gave Him something to eat. When He was thirsty, when He was a stranger, when He needed clothes, when He was sick, when He was in prison, they were there, meeting His needs. Those to the right of Jesus were there to help and bring comfort to those brothers (and sisters) of His.

But what of those to His left? The goats. I can imagine them standing there with puzzled looks on their faces. "When were You there, Lord? When did You come to us hungry, thirsty, a stranger, needing clothes, sick, and in prison? When, Lord?" Jesus' answer pierces my heart just as much today as it did the first time I read it so many years ago. "He will reply, 'I tell you the truth, whatever you did not do for one of the least of these, you did not do for me'" (verse 45).

I remember the early days of our recovery. Mona literally was screaming for someone who had made it, someone she could sit and talk with and relate to, someone who could honestly tell her that this seemingly impossible task of healing could be done. I remember sitting in the dark, holding her, trying to reassure her that everything would work out. But how could I know? I, too, needed someone with experience to talk to. Our Christian counselor was great, but he was getting paid to help us. I needed a Paul to help this Timothy get through the really tough times. Someone who had done it before me. Someone who could say, "I know," because he really did know!

Don't get me wrong, God was truly the center of our focus, but someone with skin on was a deep felt need for both Mona and me in those dark and lonely times. The hard cold truth was we could find no one.

This is the very reason I feel so compelled to write this letter to you. If you hear anything from the pages of this book, I want you to hear this: We are here for you!

If I have taken anything away from this adultery recovery process, it is the desperate crying need for people like you and me to have other people to lean on in the Lord. Jesus with skin on, if you

will. And why not? Alcoholics, drug addicts—you name the problem—have a support group of some kind. So why isn't the body of
Christ supporting those in recovery from such a dark and ugly sin?
Maybe that's just the point. I believe the church wants to pretend it
doesn't exist, and so would we.

Marital love is a tangible picture of the relationship God wants
with each one of us, the "great romance." To realize that we have
perverted the purest intimacy God provides on this earth is to begin
to comprehend the depth of the pain we've caused the Lord and
ourselves. I've heard it said that sexual sin is a rape of the Holy Spirit,
who lives in each believer. Most of us do not want to believe we
are capable of such things. Well, we are. It does happen, and Satan
is there, fully armed to persuade us that there is no hope for this
particular sin.

But God is there too. And He is capable of healing even this. We
must support brothers and sisters who are in such a horrible, hurting
mess.

I remember all too well the time our Christian counselor asked if
we remembered back in the beginning how much we needed another
couple to talk to. We both emphatically agreed. Then he asked, "Are
you ready to be that couple for someone else?" Boy, that one stopped
us dead in our tracks. To be that couple for someone else meant
admitting we had been there too. It meant removing the privacy
curtains we had in place to protect what we had saved. It meant
reopening some of our wounds, and we feared what that could mean
to us. But after long hours of discussion and prayer, Mona and I
came to this conclusion: No, we really don't want to do this, but if
this is God's will, then we will be there for the people in need whom

He puts in our path. We'll be there to deliver His message that says, "Yes, you can heal!" We'll be there to show a way to the hope and healing that come through Jesus Christ when you lay it all at His feet and allow Him to lead you through.

Of course, this is not feasible for most of you now. You are way too fresh in this process. But down the road, when the Lord prompts you, do me a favor, will you? Consider being that couple for someone else. It is so important to let God use what He has brought us through to help others. Think of how you are feeling right now. Consider it when the opportunity comes. Work diligently now so that when and if He calls you, you will be ready. You will have something to offer His children.

When the world would have you believe that there is no hope, that your marriage can never make it, be God's audible voice. When your Christian friends advise you to hang it up ("After all, it is adultery and Scripture releases you"), add to that advice the whole context of Scripture. Because, you see, God hates divorce. Stand with the Lord and your spouse; fight the good fight. Mona and I made it, and I believe you can too.

I can honestly say, as I look across the laptop screen at my wife of over thirty years, I love her more today than I ever have. We've shared our story to illustrate the reality of the journey and the reality that it can be completed. We are completely healed. We again have love and trust in our marriage. Our journey as husband and wife is not over, and it was not irrevocably ruined by this sin. God offers you and your spouse the same opportunity.

God brings us through adversity to make us into the people He wants us to be, but we must do our part, and that is to obey. Be obedient to His leading, and let Him do the rest. God will give you the wisdom and the strength to complete your journey.

May He bless you and keep you.

Gary

Gary and Mona can be reached at www.HopeAndHealing.us.

Appendix

INFORMATION TO HELP YOU ON YOUR JOURNEY

Starting on the path of adultery recovery is an unknown journey for most of us. Even if for some reason we've encountered infidelity previously, each situation is a new and different journey. If we do know others who have been through it, chances are they didn't make it and divorced, or they stayed together but everyone knows they're both unhappy. Although we hear from pastors and counselors about couples who have healed, very few of us meet them face-to-face. That is why our ministry, Hope & Healing, exists. We now know a lot of couples who have healed and are very glad they did.

How Common Is Adultery?

You can find statistics confirming that from 10 percent to 80 percent of couples will experience infidelity. That's a wide range. Why can't we get a definitive number?

The easy reason can rest with the issues about defining what adultery is in the first place. Also surveys are often skewed because the participants are volunteers and not accurate representatives of people at large. In addition, a comparative study published in the *Journal of Family Psychology* showed significant differences between interviewed answers and anonymous computer questionnaires of the same sample.[1] The same participants reported a higher incidence of infidelity on the anonymous computer questionnaires than they did in the interviews.

After looking at many studies and hearing many experts, we use 25 percent. That seems to be the lowest most commonly accepted statistic. Many experts cite double that, but we'd rather err on the low side than be accused of inflating the numbers.

That means 25 percent of couples either have experienced, are currently going through, or will encounter infidelity in their marriage. One in four.

Consider what that would look like in your church service or class. That's a lot of seats. It means you are not the only ones to go through this, even though it may feel like you are. Sadly, just like divorce statistics, the numbers don't appear to be any lower for Christians than non-Christians.

How Do We Begin?

We have been asked this question countless times as we've sat across from couples still reeling from the revelation of adultery.

Perhaps you are there right now too, trying to even comprehend what has happened to your life. Hear us loudly say *you're not alone.* There is hope. There is help.

Beginning requires only two things: *agreeing to try* and *being honest.*

Agree to Try

Can you agree to try to rebuild your marriage? Can your spouse? And if the only reason one or both of you are willing to try is because you have children, we say amen and hallelujah. Those children are reason enough. So is simply desiring to be obedient to God.

If your spouse is unwilling to try at this point, we can only encourage you to leave the door open to reconciliation. We've seen God soften some hard hearts. Use this time alone to focus on getting yourself healthy again. The injury you have sustained requires healing on a personal level also.

What does it mean to try? It means acknowledging that it is going to take time and energy and that understanding healing is a slow process. Focus on getting through each minute because sometimes that's all you can do. Consider this as if you had been in a terrible accident in which you've been injured and need time to heal. You cannot, nor should you, do "the usual." Instead, you must focus on the essentials of life: Care for the children as best you can; do what you must to make a living. But give this healing process priority.

Be Honest

The second requirement is to be honest in what you say to one another. No matter what damage you fear from being honest, it is nothing compared to the damage more lies or deceit will cause later. If we could offer only one piece of advice to the infidel, it would be to tell the *whole* truth now. The consequences you think you can avoid by withholding the whole truth are usually worse when the truth does come out later. The advantage to an infidel's being transparently honest from the beginning is the huge amount of groundwork that is laid to help rebuild the trust—groundwork that won't be destroyed by the revelation of another deception.

Transparent honesty is not just advice for the infidel. The spouse also needs to be transparently honest. Often spouses assume the infidel knows what they're thinking and feeling, especially because the emotions are so overwhelming and strong.

We remember one couple sitting on our couch, seeking some help for their journey. The wife proceeded to tell us that she didn't believe her husband wanted to work on the marriage. He looked shocked and said, "I told you I want to work on it." She then replied that he avoided her in the evenings. He said, "You don't want anything to do with me. You go into the bedroom and close the door. I thought you wanted to be alone and I was trying to give you some time."

What looks like anger or rejection may actually be fear and pain. Reactions that make perfect sense to one can make absolutely no sense to another. Saying the words "I'm hurt" or "I'm scared" can be understood much better than bursting into tears and running from the room.

Don't assume anything during this time. A person's ability to discern can definitely be affected by severe stress. Don't think your spouse knows what you're thinking or feeling if you haven't verbalized it yet.

If you both walk in truth, the work you do will have a foundation. Save your energy to focus on obeying God's instructions to speak sincerely, kindly, timely, and in love.

What Do We Do?

Again, focus on the essentials of life. You need to nourish your body. Many Hope & Healing groups comment on the effectiveness of the "adultery diet." No one is particularly hungry, much less feels like cooking. Despite having little or no appetite, try to consume adequate calories that are nutritious. We can all do with less for a few days, but we must keep up our physical strength to function.

The same is true for rest. Many have trouble sleeping, which is perfectly understandable. Yet lack of sleep definitely impairs our ability to function and cope. Emotions and perceptions are also affected. Scientific studies on drivers who were sleep deprived prove that sleep deprivation affects reaction time and driving performance as much as alcohol. We simply do not function well with little sleep.

Therefore, if your goal is to heal and work through the infidelity as efficiently as possible, sleep must be one of the factors you consider important. Don't hesitate to seek medical assistance if this is a problem for you.

Get Proper Help

Enlist some help. Adultery is huge and all of us need help from others to get through it.

We encourage you to learn about adultery recovery to help you make better choices that can significantly affect healing. What do most of the experts have to say? What is commonly accepted as the best way to heal? We wouldn't think twice about seeking specialists if we were given the diagnosis of cancer. There are some good resources out there, and you'll find those we think are most helpful on our Web site: www.HopeAndHealing.us.

We do encourage professional Christian counseling. A good counseling environment is one where both of you feel you're being heard and the counselor can be trusted. But we need to understand that counselors can differ in their approach to a couple experiencing infidelity. Dr. Shirley Glass conducted a survey of therapists at thirteen conferences regarding their beliefs about the meaning and treatment of infidelity. The results showed there is very little consensus among couple therapists about why infidelity happens and how couples should be treated.[2]

That's confusing at best and detrimental at worst, and it's why we think it's important to educate yourself. The bottom line is that whatever you do to help your healing process must work for both of you. If it works for both of you and it's biblical, legal, moral, and ethical—we say go for it. If it's not working for both of you, then find something that does. Often another solution can be found with the aid of your counselor. Explain that what you're currently doing isn't working for you and explore options that can. And if you've educated yourself, you'll have more information to share with those coming alongside you.

What Do We Tell the Kids and Our Friends and Family?

We would be in error to offer one answer for all situations. What we will caution you about, though, is that those who are close to you will know something is going on. The truth is, no matter how well you believe you can hide it from them, they will sense the undercurrent. And most of us just aren't that capable of pretending everything is okay when experiencing this kind of trauma.

What you share will be greatly influenced by the events of revelation. Whether the revelation was a public blast or a private explosion determines how far-reaching your explanation needs to be. It can be as simple as "We're having some problems and we're going to work together to solve them." But if the kids overheard some things you wish they hadn't or if there is the possibility of another person filling in the details, we suggest you be the ones to do the explaining. For the kids, make it age appropriate. Sit with them all together and assure them that what is happening has nothing to do with what they did or didn't do and that your plan is to remain a family.

The same holds true for extended family and close friends. There are some people who deserve to hear what's happened from you and not somebody else. But only you can make that determination.

Choosing what to tell and how to tell it should be a private conversation between the two of you prior to meeting with whomever. Decide what words you're going to use. Neither of you should use a word that could be inflammatory to your spouse and cause the conversation to go a different direction. Try to keep it simple yet truthful. The more of the story you share, the more of the pain you reveal, and the more of the healing process you'll later need to share with them too.

How Big an Issue Is Adultery to a Marriage?

We would probably all agree adultery is a big issue and a deep wound to the integrity of the marriage. In fact, some say it's too big and marriages cannot heal from such a betrayal. We know better now because we've seen what God can do to heal a marriage when both are willing to work together. However, we do believe it is important to understand the depth of the wound and the healing it requires.

According to therapists who treat couples, infidelity is the second most difficult relationship problem, surpassed only by domestic violence.[3] It is without question a very deep wound. In fact, revelation of adultery can be so traumatic it is often followed by symptoms of PTSD (post-traumatic stress disorder).

The National Center for PTSD describes four types of symptoms: reliving the event; avoiding situations that remind you of the event; feeling numb or uninterested in activities you used to enjoy; and feeling keyed up, always alert, and on the lookout for danger.[4] These symptoms lasting longer than a month qualify for the diagnosis of PTSD.

Unfortunately, they also describe most spouses after revelation. When we think of PTSD, so often what comes to mind are soldiers who have been to war, or those who were in New York or the Pentagon on September 11, 2001. Think about it: We would never tell soldiers or 9/11 victims to just forgive, forget, and move on. Yet, that is often verbalized to an infidel's spouse, who is also a victim of a significant trauma. Traumas of this proportion take time to heal, and those who experience them need permission to take that time.

We encourage couples to consider adultery as comparable to a death. Much of what they experience will include a grieving process. They need grace and time to heal. Many people have shared with us things they have been told such as, "The adultery has been confessed and stopped. You just need to move on. Enjoy your life. Quit obsessing." These comments are coming not only from their spouse, but also from their pastor, family, and friends. What we have seen when someone is rushed through the process is that it actually prolongs the healing.

How Long Does It Take?

You will read over and over again that "healing takes time." We all want to know just how long that time is. We have sat across from couples weary from the effort and battle, tears streaming down their faces, saying, "It's been (insert specific time here). Isn't that long enough?" The answer is "apparently not." The length of your recovery and your spouse's recovery cannot be predetermined—and most likely you will be on different time schedules.

We included a generalized recovery timeline in the final chapter to help you understand some of the normal paths recovery can take. It is not intended to put *your* recovery on a timeline but rather to help you traverse the territory with a bit more understanding. And it is important to understand that as the healing moves forward, the overall intensity decreases. The trauma you experience initially will not remain static throughout the entire healing process.

The realization that we were "fully healed" came as a surprise—a surprise that it had happened some time before. We share our story in Hope & Healing groups and recall that one night as Mona was finishing her story she added, "And I can tell you now that we are fully healed." She hadn't planned on saying that because she had never even said that to herself. But when the words came out that night, she knew they were true.

We encourage you to give up any specific timetable you may have in your brain; it will only frustrate you and be detrimental to your healing. This is a marathon, not a sprint—a journey with many twists and turns, one often fraught with setbacks. But setbacks are temporary. Enjoy each small victory. Rest when you can. And remember, as long as either of you has a need to continue working, it's not over. We can only encourage you with the fact that it is worth it. It was the most difficult journey we ever took, but one we are both so glad we completed together.

Notes

Chapter 1

1. Dave Carder, *Torn Asunder* (Chicago: Moody, 1995), 36.
2. *American Heritage Dictionary,* 4th ed., s.v. "adultery."
3. Ibid., s.v. "infidelity."
4. Shirley P. Glass, PhD, *Not "Just Friends"* (New York: Free Press, 2003), 25.

Chapter 3

1. *New Bible Dictionary,* Bible Companion Series software, s.v. "faith #682."

Chapter 7

1. Glass, 164.
2. *The Complete Word Study Old Testament* (Chattanooga, TN: AMG, 1994), s.v. "539."
3. *The Complete Word Study New Testament* (Chattanooga, TN: AMG, 1992), s.v. "4103."
4. *Funk & Wagnalls Standard Dictionary,* International Ed., s.v. "faithful."
5. Donald R. Harvey, *Surviving Betrayal: Counseling an Adulterous Marriage* (Grand Rapids, MI: Baker, 1995), 201.

Chapter 8

1. Glass, 205.

2. Carder, 120.
3. Harvey, 164–65.
4. Joe and Michelle Williams, *Yes, Your Marriage Can Be Saved* (Carol Stream, IL: Tyndale, 2007), 89.

Chapter 9
1. *Funk & Wagnalls Standard Dictionary,* International Ed., s.v. "forgive."
2. Bible Companion Series, *Vine's Lexicon,* s.v. "863."
3. Charles F. Stanley, *The Gift of Forgiveness* (Nashville: Thomas Nelson, 1991), 2.
4. Beth Moore, *Breaking Free* (Nashville: Lifeway, 1999), 104.

Chapter 10
1. Dr. Douglas E. Rosenau, *A Celebration of Sex* (Nashville: Thomas Nelson, 2002), 348.
2. C. S. Lewis, *The Four Loves* (Orlando: Harcourt, 1960), 121.

Chapter 11
1. Jerry B. Jenkins, *Hedges: Loving Your Marriage Enough to Protect It* (Brentwood, TN: Wolgemuth & Hyatt, 1989), 62.
2. Glass, 35.

Chapter 12
1. Shirley P. Glass, PhD, "Shattered Vows: Getting Beyond Betrayal," *Psychology Today,* July–August 1998.
2. Glass, *Not "Just Friends,"* 31.
3. Ibid., 33.
4. Marriage Quotes at Great-Inspirational-Quotes, www.great-inspirational-quotes.com/marriage-quotes.html.

Chapter 13
1. "Fight or Flight Response: The Nerves Behind the Pain Relief," *Medical News Today,* www.medicalnewstoday.com/articles/111150.php.
2. Carder, 117.

3. Mayo Clinic, "Grief: Coping with reminders after a loss," www.mayoclinic.com/health/grief/MH00036.

Appendix

1. Tara Parker-Pope, "Love, Sex and the Changing Landscape of Infidelity," *New York Times,* October 28, 2008.
2. Glass, *Not "Just Friends,"* 5.
3. Ibid., 9.
4. National Center for PTSD, "What Is PTSD?" www.ptsd.va.gov/public/pages/what-is-ptsd.asp.

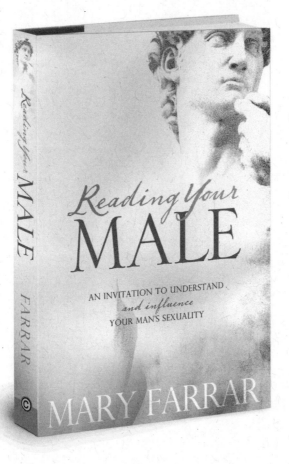